The
Hedgehog

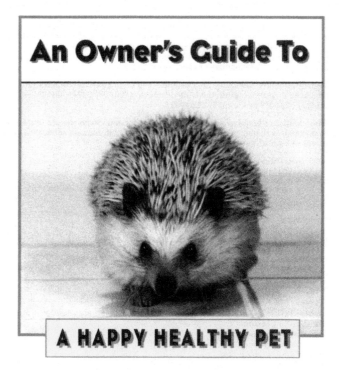

An Owner's Guide To

A HAPPY HEALTHY PET

Howell Book House

Wiley Publishing, Inc.

Howell Book House

Published by Wiley Publishing, Inc., Hoboken, NJ
Published simultaneously in Canada

Limit of Liability/Disclaimer of Warranty: While the publisher and the author have used their best efforts in preparing this book, they make no representations or warranties with respect to the accuracy or completeness of the contents of this book and specifically disclaim any implied warranties of merchantability or fitness for a particular purpose. No warranty may be created or extended by sales representatives or written sales materials. The advice and strategies contained herein may not be suitable for your situation. You should consult with a professional where appropriate. Neither the publisher nor the author shall be liable for any loss of profit or any other commercial damages, including but not limited to special, incidental, consequential, or other damages.

For general information about our other products and services, please contact our Customer Care Department within the United States at (800) 762-2974, outside the United States at (317) 572-3993 or fax (317) 572-4002.

Wiley also publishes its books in a variety of electronic formats. Some content that appears in print may not be available in electronic books. For more information about Wiley products, visit our web site at www.wiley.com.

Library of Congress Cataloging-in-Publication data

Wrobel, Dawn.
The hedgehog: an owner's guide to happy, healthy pet/by Dawn Wrobel with Susan A. Brown, DVM.
p.cm.
Includes bibliographical references
ISBN: 978-1-63026-041-5
1. Hedgehogs as pets. I. Title. II. Series
SF459.H43W76   1996, 2002
636.9'332—dc21   96-49686
                                  CIP
ISBN 978-1-63026-205-1
Manufactured in the United States of America

10 9 8 7

Series Director: Kira Sexton
Book Design: Michele Laseau
Cover Design: Michael Freeland
Photography Editor: Richard Fox
Illustration: Jeff Yesh
Photography:
  Cover photos by Renee Stockdale (front) and Jean Wentworth (back)
  Joan Balzarini: 5, 6, 22, 26, 28, 36, 65, 70, 106, 113
  Bob Mason: 25, 32, 40, 55, 57, 58, 59, 60, 64
  John Shilling: 109
  Renee Stockdale: 2–3, 7, 8, 9, 11, 12, 14, 17, 18, 19, 20, 21, 23, 24, 26, 27,
    29, 31, 38–39, 41, 42, 44, 45, 46, 47, 54, 61, 62, 66, 67, 71, 74, 76, 78, 81,
    82, 83, 88–89, 90, 91, 92, 95, 96, 97, 99, 103, 104, 107, 108, 110, 115, 117
  Jean Wentworth: 53, 100, 119
  Dawn Wrobel: 24, 30, 37, 50, 56, 68, 98, 101, 111
Page creation by: Wiley Indianapolis Composition Services

Contents

Welcome
to the
World

of the

Hedgehog

External Features of the Hedgehog

Muzzle

Nose

Ear

Eye

Neck

Toes

Spines
(Quills)

Underside
(Belly)

Back

Tail

What
Is a
Hedgehog?

A scientist would say that a hedgehog belongs to the class known as *Mammals.* Their subclass, *Eutheria,* includes the higher mammals as opposed to marsupials or egg-laying mammals. Within the subclass *Eutheria,* hedgehogs belong to the order *Insectivora,* which also includes moles, tenrecs and shrews. This order contains the earliest examples of placental mammals—mammals whose young are retained within the mother's uterus and nourished via a placenta before

birth. The hedgehog family is *Erinaceidae,* which also includes moon rats, gymnures and shrew hedgehogs. This family is the most primitive living insectivore family. Fossils of hedgehog ancestors date back to the time of the dinosaurs. Finally, the subfamily or genus that includes only spiny hedgehogs is *Erinaceinae.* Some authorities prefer to place them in the genus *Atelerix,* and it is this name that you will see most frequently in books about African Pygmy hedgehogs.

Origins of the African Pygmy Hedgehog

We know that hedgehogs have been inhabiting the earth as long as the dinosaurs, but in order to understand the needs of the hedgehog as a pet today, it is important to learn something about the hedgehog's natural habitat. The African hedgehog, commonly referred to as the African Pygmy hedgehog, is found across a large area of hot, dry land stretching from southern Europe all the way to South Africa, and from Senegal to northern Somalia, thus covering most of Africa. It is a creature of the savanna, an area of grassland interspersed with thick brush and occasional stands of trees. The territory of a single hedgehog is a circle with a radius of about 650 to 1,000 feet around its burrow. This territory may be even larger during periods when food is scarce.

This modern hedgehog, like most mammals, enjoys some playtime.

EVOLUTIONARY LINK TO HUMANS?

Although hedgehogs are very primitive mammals and their development diverged from that of Homo Sapiens millennia ago, there is an interesting connection between the two. Researchers at two universities have discovered that the blood of both the European and African hedgehogs contains a lipoprotein identical to one of those found in human blood. This lipoprotein contributes to the formation of clots that cause heart attacks. In the past, this particular lipoprotein was only found in humans and a few nonhuman primates. Research is presently being conducted and our prickly little friends may eventually contribute a solution to a human health problem.

A close-up of hedgehog quills resembles a stack of finely packed needles.

Hedgehog Appearance

Knowledge of the origins of the hedgehog may be useful in understanding how hedgehogs can be studied in our present-day environment. The pet owner will most likely encounter hedgehogs that come from one of the two major categories: the European hedgehog and the African hedgehog. The European hedgehog is the larger hedgehog of the two types. It may grow to 12 inches in length and 3 pounds in weight. Typically, both the fur and the quills are a chestnut brown color. European hedgehogs are a protected species throughout much of their range because they are unfortunately the victims of a dwindling natural habitat. These adult hedgehogs are especially valued by gardeners who often try to attract them to their gardens because they may consume up to one-third of their body weight in slugs, snails and insects in a single day. European hedgehogs are rarely seen in zoos or the pet trade in the United States and Canada.

The African hedgehog, in contrast to its European relatives, averages about 1 pound in weight and 6 to 9 inches in length. Weight range is from 11 to 20 ounces in healthy individuals. The normal color seen in these hedgehogs is a white or cream colored belly and face with white quills banded in black or brown. The exact scientific names vary depending on the reference work and they are most often referred to collectively as *Atelerix albiventris*, or the Pruner's hedgehog, in pet books. It is this charming little creature with the big name that is the focus of this book.

Because hedgehogs are naturally inquisitive, they are often depicted as whimsical figures in children's stories.

The face, legs and underside of the hedgehog are covered in soft fur that is usually white in color. The face may be masked in a darker color and the lower leg often exhibits darker coloring. The hedgehog's eyes are large, dark and bright in healthy animals. Its ears are typically shorter than the quills, and are rounded and covered with fine hairs. The hedgehog has five toes on the front feet and four on the back.

HEDGEHOG TERMS

Hedgehogs are part of the *Mammal* class, but come from the earliest living insectivore family, *Erinaceidae*. This family is part of the *Insectivora* order, which is included in the *Eutheria* subclass.

Male and female hedgehogs look basically the same in color and fur texture. If you are not sure what sex it is, there are a couple of easy ways to investigate. You will find that females have four to five sets of tiny nipples and the anal and vaginal openings are adjacent to each other, next to the ½-inch long tail. In males, the opening of the prepuce, which houses the penis, is in the middle of the lower abdomen.

A Prickly Defense

The hedgehog is designed to thwart all but the most persistent predator. Quills are modified, hollowed hairs. They are typically "agouti," or banded, with a white tip and base and a center band of black or brown. This mottled pattern acts as camouflage for the hedgehog so it can blend in with its surroundings. The spines or quills vary from ½ to 1 inch on adult hedgehogs. The length and density of

quills vary from one hedgehog to another. In addition, the hedgehog's strong muscles run in a circle around the body under its loose skin. This muscle pattern allows the hedgehog to draw its body into a tight ball with erect, crisscross quills for defense.

This African Pygmy hedgehog, rolled up into a ball, is protected by its quills.

Color Variations

Due to captive breeding, there is a great increase in the variety of quill colors that now exists. The foundation stock for domestic hedgehogs was initially of two predominant patterns. The hedgehogs commonly known as Pruner's hedgehogs had black and white quills, a dark mask and legs and a wide division in the quills between the ears. The Algerian hedgehogs had brown and cream colored quills with no mask.

The most common color patterns are salt and pepper or agouti, snowflake and cinnamon. The three terms "normal," "agouti" and "salt and pepper" are used interchangeably to refer to hedgehogs with black and white or brown and cream quills. Agouti simply means that a single hair, or in this case, quill, contains more than one color. Salt and pepper usually refers to the original color of the pure species *albiventrix,* or Pruner's hedgehog.

Chocolate is the original color of the pure species *algerian,* with quills of dark brown and cream and no facial mask. Algerian hedgehogs have been used to develop many of the lighter colors of hedgehogs.

Snowflake hedgehogs have the most controversial set of color descriptions. Depending on the breeder or association, snowflake might refer to a hedgehog with 100 percent all white quills, no mask and normal, dark pigment on the nose and eyes. Others define snowflake as 75 percent or more all white quills with no mask. If a hedgehog is advertised as "snowflake," be sure to ask for a more detailed description so that you know just what snowflake means to the breeder or store you are working with.

Panda hedgehogs have white or almost all white quills with dark eyes and nose, plus a dark mask and dark ears.

Cinnamon hedgehogs typically have cream colored quills with a light brown or reddish brown band, a light face and light legs. This color has also been called blonde, champagne, rose beige and apricot. Animals often have a light brown or pinkish nose, rather than a black nose. I describe a hedgehog with this coloring as one that looks like the color of coffee with a lot of cream.

Fawn is used to refer to a cinnamon hedgehog with a dark mask and sometimes dark legs. This is a more unusual pattern.

Mocha hedgehogs have chocolate brown and cream quills with a dark mask. When this color has a gray cast, it is often called mud. It is sometimes the result of a cross between a pure *algerian* and a pure *albiventrix* hedgehog.

LITERARY HEDGEHOGS

Besides foretelling an additional six weeks of winter, hedgehogs are a favorite subject for folktales and children's stories. Look for hedgehogs in: Beatrix Potter's *Mrs. Tiggywinkle,* Lewis Carroll's *Alice in Wonderland* and the fable *The Hare and the Hedgehog.* The queen in *Alice in Wonderland* used a rolled up hedgehog as a croquet ball!

Cream hedgehogs have off-white or ivory quills, no mask and ruby eyes. The eye color is very important as it is darker than the pink eyes of an albino, but definitely red when compared to a normal hedgehog. It is often hard to tell whether or not a cream hedgehog is an albino as a baby. The deciding factor when the eyes open is whether the eyes are pink or red.

Some hedgehogs, like this resourceful pet, have "salt and pepper" quill coloring.

Smoke point or silver point hedgehogs have quills that are distinctly white and pale gray with the overall appearance being pale to smoky gray. Usually, they have a facial mask and dark legs. This is a definite gray color, not black or chocolate.

Albino hedgehogs are true albinos. They have white or off-white quills with pink eyes and a liver-colored or pink nose. They have no pigment anywhere. Albinos are rumored to have shorter life spans than other hedgehogs. This is true in the wild because the white color does not afford the same protection and camouflage as the standard agouti quill. In captivity, with proper care, albinos live just as long as their pigmented relatives.

Spotted, or pinto, hedgehogs can be any base color with one or more white or cream colored spots. Rounded spots on the two sides are the most common spotting pattern followed by a pattern with a stripe of white across the rear end.

As time goes on, selective breeding will probably result in additional colors and eventually in standardization of the color definitions.

Hedgehog Personality and Peculiar Habits

The hedgehog has a number of habits that seem unusual to many people. These habits should be taken into consideration by the potential hedgehog owner. Some habits are merely interesting, some affect the suitability of the hedgehog as a pet, and some habits, such as self-anointing, can send a new hedgehog owner running needlessly for medical help when the animal is merely demonstrating one of its peculiar traits.

This studious hedgehog is posing proudly next to its scientific name, Atelerix albiventris.

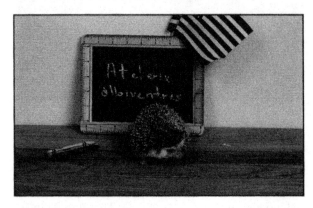

ROLLING IN A BALL

The defensive posture of rolling into a tight, quill-covered ball is one of the most memorable traits of the hedgehog. It was used to advantage by Lewis Carroll in his work *Alice in Wonderland.* In this novel, the mad queen used hedgehogs for the balls in a game of croquet. The hedgehog forms itself into a ball by means of the longitudinal *orbicularis* and *panniculus carnosus* muscles running around the body. These muscles act like a drawstring that pulls the skin around the sides and down over the feet and head so that the hedgehog becomes a tight little ball of spines. The spines can be moved individually by a complex layer of muscles beneath the loose skin. The hedgehog assumes this position when it hears loud or sharp noises, smells a potential predator, when touched by another animal or often when an unfamiliar human attempts to pick up the hedgehog.

The spines or quills are used as a defense by even the tamest of hedgehogs. A pet hedgehog that is caressed over the back will sometimes erect only his forehead spines if the strokes move too close to the face or chin. Even young unweaned hedgehogs will keep their forehead spines pulled over the eyes during play.

Hedgehogs also sleep rolled in a ball, but there is a noticeable difference between this resting ball and the ball of defense. When resting, the animal is only partly rolled up, breathes slowly and deeply and the quills are generally relaxed. When frightened, all the spines are erect for protection and the breathing is noisy and rapid.

SELF-ANOINTING AND THE FLEHMEN RESPONSE

Hedgehogs can occasionally foam at the mouth. This delights children and worries adults. This process, called "self-anointing" or "anting," is triggered by new or unusual scents in the hedgehog's cage or on its handler. Scents can include a variety of things, including food, furniture, leather, another hedgehog, the hedgehog's own feces or perfume. The hedgehog will lick and sometimes even chew on the scented object, then produce large amounts of frothy saliva. The hedgehog will then turn its head back and spread the saliva on its back and flanks with its long tongue. Some hedgehogs self-anoint frequently, others rarely perform this behavior. It is a most unusual act to watch and may be frightening to new owners if they have not been informed about this odd behavior.

No one is sure what the purpose of self-anointing is, but it may be a way of making the hedgehog's quills more effective weapons by coating them with toxic substances. Some people experience an itching or

burning sensation after handling hedgehogs; this may
be due to the saliva coating the quills. Some experts
think that the purpose of this behavior is part of the
hedgehog's mating ritual, that perhaps it acts like a
perfume to attract members of the opposite sex.
Others believe it is an attempt on the part of the
hedgehog to smell like other objects in its environment for purposes of self-defense. The saliva will carry
the scent of the chewed substance and allow the hedgehog to blend in with the scent of its surroundings.

*Hedgehogs some-
times self-anoint
if placed on
something with a
new smell, such
as a blanket.*

Whatever the reason, this particular habit may also
have led to the unsubstantiated belief that hedgehogs
frequently are afflicted with rabies. Self-anointing
hedgehogs may have been unjustly confused with some
rabid animals that produce excessive, frothy saliva.

In addition to self-anointing, hedgehogs, when scent-
ing or tasting, may hold their nose high in the air, the
mouth slightly opened and the upper lip curled in
a curious gesture. This shows that the hedgehog is
smelling something interesting or dangerous and
is being extremely attentive to its surroundings. This
posture, similar to that seen in dogs and horses, is
known as the flehmen response.

HEDGEHOG NOISES

Hedgehogs produce a variety of noises. The most frequently noticed and most characteristic noise is the

"huffing" or "snuffling" sound they make as they go about the business of searching for food or rearranging their cage. They sometimes make this sound when being handled, as well as when two strange hedgehogs are put together in the same cage or playpen. Many people compare this noise to the sound of a freight train locomotive.

At feeding time the hedgehog will emit a series of soft grunts that ranges from a sniffing sound to louder, almost pig-like grunts that may be difficult to discern over the loud crunch of the dry food in its bowl.

When a hedgehog is upset, frightened or agitated, it will make a loud hissing sound. This is usually accompanied by a jumping or "popping" motion when the animal is very upset. The hedgehog will also emit a clicking noise just at the moment it jumps. The jump or "pop" will drive the quills into an attacker if the hiss is not enough to warn it off.

Baby hedgehogs make a quite different noise. It resembles the chirp of small birds. The sound of chirps is often the first indication that there are new babies in a nest. Babies will continue to chirp for about four weeks. As the baby hedgehogs get older, the chirp gradually changes to a cry. The cry usually disappears shortly after the baby hedgehog's eyes open and it begins to move about on its own.

Screams and loud, high-pitched squeals are signs that something is seriously wrong and should be investigated immediately. Hedgehogs that are fighting, trapped or injured can emit surprisingly loud screams. Hedgehogs are active climbers and they can get caught on a cage or a water bottle holder or stuck trying to escape. If you have more than one hedgehog in a cage, screams may be a sign that a fight is taking place and that you need to separate the hedgehogs immediately.

Hedgehogs may emit a variety of sounds when handled by their human caretakers. When startled, hedgehogs emit a hissing, huffing noise and may even "pop" when handled. Relaxed hedgehogs typically make soft, snuffling sounds as they crawl around on their owners, just as they would while foraging in the wild. The occasional hedgehog may even purr like a cat. The purr is a pleasant sound and signals a very contented pet.

HEDGEHOGS AND TOXINS

It is widely reported that hedgehogs are immune or highly resistant to many toxins that might kill humans or other animals. However, research on this subject is limited and pet owners should be careful to keep disinfectants, insect sprays, rodent poisons and other toxic materials out of reach of their pets.

SOCIAL LIFE

The average hedgehog has very little social life and is generally a solitary creature. In the wild, hedgehogs normally come together only to mate. They are not territorial in the sense of defending a fixed area of land, but they do keep their distance from each other. One study indicated that members of the same sex chose to remain 60 feet apart. When males meet in the search for willing females, fierce fighting can erupt until the loser retreats. It is never advisable to house two male hedgehogs together.

Groups of female hedgehogs under captive conditions can be more social and gregarious if they have plenty of space and more than one hiding area. However, it may appear that two females are getting along fine, then one day some source of conflict triggers fierce fighting. Serious injuries can result. A problem with community housing in hedgehogs is that the animals must share food. Often, the more aggressive eater will become obese because the pet owner must provide adequate food to ensure that the less dominant of the two animals is adequately fed.

NOCTURNAL INSTINCTS

The hedgehog is a nocturnal creature, meaning it sleeps all day and becomes active at dusk to forage for food. Throughout the night you will most likely find the domesticated hedgehog running on an exercise wheel. The hedgehog has a generally casual style about how it acquires food, but it is quite speedy if and when the need should arise. Such instances are if the hedgehog is in pursuit of prey or is fearful of becoming prey. If necessary, the hedgehog will exhibit a burst of speed as fast as 6 feet per second! In addition to their adaptability to the environment, hedgehogs also have the ability to swim. This gives them another advantage over possible predators, since not all animals are capable of maneuvering on both the land and the water. They look quite harmless, but if disturbed while foraging, the hedgehog will roll itself into a ball and begin to snort, hiss or growl. This same behavior is exhibited in pet shops when the animals are handled by strangers or taken to new surroundings. An overly defensive hedgehog will not make the best pet to bring home, as you spend more time with a ball of quills than interacting with your pet.

A log in an aquarium makes a fine spot for your hedgehog to nap, especially when followed by a good stretch!

REST REQUIREMENTS

During periods of cold weather when the temperature drops below 45 degrees Fahrenheit, hedgehogs will go into a period of dormancy or hibernation. They may also *aestivate* during periods of extremely high temperature. Aestivation is a period of hot weather dormancy, but is not a true hibernation. This is another physiological means that the hedgehog has to cope with environmental stress.

17

During the day, the hedgehog sleeps in its burrow, which may be at the base of a bush, under a pile of rocks or in a termite mound (all of which keep it cool and comfortable).

FAVORITE FOODS

Although zoologically classed as insectivores, hedgehogs are certainly not confined to a diet of insects. They are opportunistic feeders who will take almost anything edible that comes along. In many areas, the loss of habitat has forced them into the fringes of populated areas where they have learned to adapt to a different food supply. During the early days of importation, many hedgehogs were trapped in or near garbage dumps. Although they have the ability to travel rapidly for short distances, they are not generally fast enough to catch healthy prey that have better endurance for a long run. For this reason, they serve an important part in the natural food chain by consuming injured or sick animals. Due to this great variety of acceptable foods, it is not often necessary for the hedgehog to travel great distances for a meal.

Be sure to offer your hedgehog a varied diet for good health. Mealworms are one nutritious snack to consider.

African hedgehogs, like their European cousins, may eat as much as one-third of their own body weight in food each night. Small prey are simply bitten to death. When making a meal of a snake, the hedgehog will break the back of the snake first before beginning to eat.

It is often helpful to consider an animal's diet in order to understand the structure of its mouth. Hedgehogs have a healthy appetite for food items that require holding and crushing; therefore, the arrangement of teeth is designed for this type of diet. Hedgehog teeth are primitive, with the front incisors being longer than the remaining teeth. There are typically 36 teeth in adult hedgehogs. Pet owners will typically be able to see only the front incisors unless they catch their pet during a yawn.

Hedgehogs have the spatial ability to follow a maze made by tubes.

SMARTS AND SENSES

The brain of a hedgehog is small and primitive compared to other mammals their size. Generally the mammals this size will have a brain with more convolutions, indicating greater intellectual development. In comparison, the hedgehog's brain has few convolutions. However, hedgehogs have excellent olfactory, auditory and tactile powers, as well as a good sense of smell and hearing; therefore, these areas of the brain are well developed. They sport long bristle-like hairs around their mouth and nose that are extremely sensitive and convey information about the hedgehog's environment. Hedgehogs also have an organ that is specialized to sense heat. Poor eyesight and limited ability to recognize color are their main weaknesses.

19

*The legs of this
hedgehog are
strong and agile,
helping it get
down from pre-
carious positions.*

PEAK PERFORMERS

Contrary to the initial impression of a slow, short-legged animal that one might get, hedgehogs are good all-around performers. They have a mechanical power output, per unit of body weight, similar to some of the much larger mammals with specialized limbs, such as the dog. When an undisturbed hedgehog is walking or running, it has a leggy appearance and the belly is raised clear of the ground. N. C. Heglund, a hedgehog researcher studying the mechanics of locomotion in primitive mammals, reported hedgehogs running at speeds up to 9 kilometers per hour. In addition, they are strong climbers and can dig quite powerfully with their front limbs.

LIFE SPAN

In the wild, it is thought that the typical life span for an African hedgehog is eighteen to twenty-four months. The "pygmy" varieties have a documented life span of seven years in captivity, although the life span for the average pet is four to six years of age.

Hedgehogs
as **Pets**

The vast majority of hedgehog owners will tell you that they purchased their pets because they were incredibly cute or too fascinating to resist. Although increasingly available in pet stores, they are still a rare pet. They are also very unusual, with a fur covered face and underside and sharp quills on their back. Living with a hedgehog is an opportunity to be in contact with an animal that has survived without evolutionary changes for millions of years.

They are interesting to observe, nonaggressive, relatively easy to care for, have no body scent of any significance and make very little noise. Unlike larger exotic pets, a hedgehog can live a healthy life within

the confines of a high-rise apartment. They do, however, require a patient, gentle and relaxed owner.

Who Should Own a Hedgehog?

Hedgehogs are primarily a pet for adults, teenagers or
older children with good animal skills. Very few people
are allergic to hedgehogs, so they are an excellent
choice for people who enjoy animals but may have

allergies to pets such as cats and
dogs. Although they appreciate a
regular playtime, they can adapt to
owners who have irregular sched-
ules. A potential hedgehog owner
must be willing to commit to caring
for the pet for a minimum of six
years.

Due to their physical design,
hedgehogs are not suitable pets
for small children. Young children
may have trouble hanging on to
an active hedgehog. If the child
squeezes the hedgehog in an

*These children
can safely handle
hedgehogs because
they have learned
how to treat these
sensitive pets
properly.*

attempt to hang on to it, the hedgehog will most likely
put out its quills in defense and stick the child, or it
may even resort to a bite. When this happens, children
will usually drop the hedgehog, which can result in
injury to the pet or the development of a fear of being
handled.

Traits to Consider

Hedgehogs have distinct personality traits that need
to be addressed before you decide to make this pet
a part of your household. The hedgehogs found in
the United States as pets are descendants of hedgehogs imported from Africa, including E. algirus and
A. albiventris. Occasionally, an Egyptian long-eared
hedgehog will show up as a pet. Although these hedgehogs have been domestically raised for several genera-
tions, they have not been domesticated long enough to
lose their characteristic lifestyle.

PERSONALITY

A hedgehog litter may include from one to seven babies. Just as a litter of puppies will have a bully and its more submissive puppy, a litter of hedgehogs can include both outgoing, inquisitive hoglets and shy, withdrawn hoglets. Pick a hedgehog that suits your own idea of the perfect hedgehog pet. Do you want a pet that will only be comfortable sitting in your lap, or one that will lead you on adventures?

The most important factor in selecting a hedgehog other than health is the personality of your future pet. Hedgehogs, like any other animal, come in a range of personalities, and hedgehogs from a single litter can exhibit the same range of temperaments present in a litter of puppies. Some are very outgoing, may be awakened easily during the day and will come looking for their owners when spoken to softly. These are the hedgehogs that may also be the most active and inquisitive pets. Typically, it is hard to get them to roll into a ball and very hard to keep them still.

A hedgehog that takes to being handled and is outgoing will enjoy play activities, such as rolling in a ball.

BURNING THE MIDNIGHT OIL

It is important to understand a little about this lifestyle in order to decide if a hedgehog is a suitable pet for your home and family. The first thing to consider is that the hedgehog is basically nocturnal. A pet hedgehog will wake up when the sun goes down and become very active in its cage or on an exercise wheel from sundown until dawn. Most do NOT like to be awakened during the daytime and may even become aggressive and bite if subjected to daytime handling. If you are looking for a pet that you can play with during the day,

*This outgoing
hedgehog likes
to ham it up in
front of the
camera.*

this is NOT the pet for you unless you are willing to gradually change the feeding and handling schedule to encourage your pet to become more active during daylight hours.

LITTLE BALLS OF ENERGY

The second thing that a potential hedgehog owner needs to understand is that hedgehogs need a great deal of exercise. A hedgehog in the wild covers a territory 650 to 1,000 feet in diameter every day in search of food. These animals run on instinct, and cannot be disciplined as you would a dog or a cat. Put a hedgehog in a 10- or 20-gallon aquarium with no exercise and he will likely become fat and/or difficult to handle. Hedgehogs need a large cage so they have space for exercise. You have to make a commitment to providing adequate exercise for your pet if you are to enjoy a pleasant and healthy relationship.

*Hedgehogs love
to run on an
exercise wheel
and will do so
all night long.*

The third consideration is that although most hedgehogs live to be four to six years old, occasionally one lives to the ripe old age of nine or ten. Are you ready to provide comfort and care for your pet for that period of time? On the other hand, if you are tired of short-lived pets, the longer life span of the African hedgehog is definitely a factor in their favor.

A plastic "kiddy pool" makes a safe and spacious area for play and exercise.

BONDING

Hedgehogs must be well socialized with friends and family. A socialized hedgehog will rarely erect its quills and will generally accept handling by anyone, although occasionally a hedgehog without contact with people other than its owner will bond strictly with the owner. An unsocialized hedgehog will erect its spines, hiss, jump, and occasionally even nip. Although hedgehogs are not social animals in the wild, as pets they respond positively to quiet handling, touching, verbal communication and attention. You also should respect that a hedgehog needs quiet time alone.

CARING FOR A UNIQUE PET

There are also other considerations due to the fact that hedgehogs are still relatively rare pets. Veterinarians with experience in treating sick or injured hedgehogs are even more rare. Although your pet may never need veterinary care, it's a good thing to investigate the availability of medical care before purchasing such an unusual pet. It may be necessary to drive a great distance for qualified veterinary care. In some areas, it is difficult to locate pet sitters willing to care for hedge-hogs. Do you have someone reliable who can care for your pet when you are on vacation? Hedgehogs do best when left in their own homes during vacation periods, provided a reliable person checks on them daily and provides food, water and attention.

A confident hedgehog won't mind being held by its owner.

If you have allergies, hedgehogs may be an excellent pet for you since they rarely shed hair or dander. However, household members with aller-gies may be allergic to some of the bed-ding used for hedge-hogs. You may need to take additional care to provide bedding and litter material that are acceptable to the hedgehog and not harmful to the health of family members.

A baseline weight should be taken at your hedgehog's first visit to the veterinarian.

If you have other pets in your home, you need to be aware that dogs and cats may consider hedgehogs as prey, and ferrets may consider them as toys because they are interesting, small and fast moving. You must provide your pet hedgehog with an enclosure that is safe from other household pets.

A Reminder About Commitment

As a caged pet, hedgehogs require less care and attention than a dog or cat and can adapt easily

to apartment living. However, hedgehogs are still living creatures and require attention to their particular needs. When you purchase a hedgehog, you are making a commitment that will typically last four to six years, and perhaps as long as ten years. You will be responsible for your pet's food, housing, medical care and exercise for a number of years, and you need to consider the investment carefully before making a hedgehog part of your household.

This dog, naturally curious about his new housemate, needs supervision.

27

Choosing and Preparing for Your Hedgehog

Once you have made an informed decision to purchase a hedgehog, it is time to investigate where to find one. If you live in a city, you can start by contacting the local pet stores. Chances are one of them will carry hedgehogs in stock or will have a contract to obtain hedgehogs from a breeder or broker.

Things to Look for in Your New Hedgehog

ABOUT HAND GENTLING

An important quality to look for is if the hedgehog has been hand gentled. An animal that has been hand gentled should unroll on your arm and begin to relax its quills soon after you pick it up. Animals that have not been gentled will remain in a ball with their quills erect.

THE BREEDER OPTION

If you live in a rural area, you will probably need to order your hedgehog from a breeder. One advantage of purchasing a hedgehog from a breeder is that you may be able to obtain hedgehogs with more unusual coloring—such as cream, cinnamon, albino or spotted hedgehogs. A list of breeders may be obtained by writing to the associations listed in the resources chapter. If there are no breeders in your area, purchasing a hedgehog from a breeder may become more expensive than purchasing a hedgehog from a local pet store because you will incur additional charges for air freight, a shipping kennel, health certificate and transportation to an airport.

EVALUATING HEALTH

If you are comfortable with the hedgehog's reaction to you, begin to examine it more closely. The **eyes** should be clear, bright and free of any cloudiness or sign of injury. The **nose** should be dry or slightly moist and free of any discharge. **Ears** should be erect and clean. Watch for ragged edges on the ears in a young hedgehog as this can be a sign of a mite or fungal infection. The **fur** on the legs, face and underbelly should be

soft and in good condition. There should be no sores, crusting or swelling of the skin and no bald patches of hair. While examining the belly, check to see that the **rectal and genital areas** are clean and free of moisture and fecal material. There should be no caked material or staining that might have resulted from diarrhea. The pads on the **feet** should feel soft, but firm on a young hedgehog. A missing toe is of little consequence to a pet as long as the wound that caused it is healed.

A knowledgeable staff will be able to provide health and care tips, and help you decide on appropriate supplies and a cage.

Healthy Skin

Next, part the quills and examine the skin. Watch for excessive dry skin flakes that may indicate inflammation or external parasites. The quill coat should be even and free of bald spots. Hedgehogs lose occa-

sional quills as a normal renewal process, just as hair on other animals and humans is replaced. You should not observe excessive quill loss all at once or bald areas. The exception is in growing baby hoglets. As hedgehogs grow they go through several sets of quills. Do not mistake the shedding of the tiny, sharp baby quills for a sign of ill health. Playing with a healthy weanling may result in the shedding of a dozen quills in your lap.

The healthy hedgehog should have ample fur on its legs, face and underbelly.

If your young hedgehog is losing quills, but has clear skin and is not scratching, this quill loss is probably just a normal molt. If your hedgehog has flaky skin, open sores or is scratching constantly, it may have external parasites or other skin disease and should be taken to a veterinarian.

Warning Signs

Next, observe the hedgehog as it moves around. It should move without signs of a limp. The hedgehog should not be sneezing, wheezing or coughing. It is abnormal for a hedgehog to be scratching itself excessively. Does the hedgehog have an offensive odor? Is the hedgehog free of any cuts, abrasions or unusual lumps? Examine the cage for fecal material that is firm. It should not be watery, green or streaked with blood. Never buy a hedgehog that shows any signs of

---

PET STORE SPECIFICS . . .

Before you decide to purchase your hedgehog from a pet store, make sure the store conforms to some essential standards. Look for clean cages, a nesting box for the hedgehogs, plenty of food and clean water, a variety of supplies for hedgehogs, healthy hedgehogs that have been treated for internal and external parasites, breeder information and tip sheets on health and care.

sickness or one that is in a very dirty cage as it may become sick later. The stress of moving to a new home can lower the hedgehog's resistance to disease so you want to make sure you start out with a clean, healthy animal. Once you know what temperament you are looking for and how to recognize a healthy animal, the next thing to consider is the age and sex of the hedgehog.

MALE OR FEMALE?

Hedgehogs of either sex make suitable pets. Some people think that females tame more readily than males, and others think that males make the most interesting pets. There is no musky odor to either sex, as in some other pets, although the urine from males may smell slightly stronger than the females'. If the cages are kept clean and you are careful about your hedgehog's diet, you should never have an odor problem. Female hedgehogs do not go

through a regularly scheduled reproductive cycle like some other mammals and therefore do not experience the temperament changes related to cycling. Males are not overly aggressive, except with other males.

The hedgehog's cage should be clean and free from strong odor and feces.

One point in favor of male hedgehogs is that they are usually less expensive to purchase than female hedgehogs. Breeding programs typically use only one male to every four or five females, thus creating a surplus of male hedgehogs.

There is, however, one potential problem if you purchase a female hedgehog: It may be pregnant. Although hedgehogs do not mature until six months of age, they become sexually active as early as seven weeks of age. Many pet stores and some inexperienced breeders do not separate the male and female weanlings. Consequently, pet owners unknowingly may bring home a pregnant pet.

31

Determining Sex

Before taking your hedgehog home, have someone help you check to make certain you know the sex of the animal. To do this, hold the hedgehog on its back. If it is a female, the anal and vaginal openings will be adjacent to each other with no space in between. If it is a male, the prepuce that covers the penis has an opening in the middle of the abdomen that looks like a pink button. Do not confuse the tiny pink tail located near the anal opening close to the quills with the penis. If you cannot observe the animal with its belly up, try holding it over a mirror or setting it on a clear glass dish or container.

Male and female hedgehogs are sexually active after they are seven weeks old. Keep your hedgehogs separated to prevent a litter of hoglets.

Separate Cages Are Best

Hedgehogs are solitary animals in the wild and it is not necessary to have more than one hedgehog as a pet. They do not keep each other company, as horses or dogs would. If you decide to purchase more than one hedgehog, they will probably need separate cages. It is nearly impossible to keep two male hedgehogs together once they are more than three months old, although it is occasionally possible to keep two females together in a large enclosure with more than one nest box. If you house a male and female together, the male WILL attempt to breed the female, then will happily eat the babies when they are born.

32

Many people feel that hedgehogs should be purchased at a very young age, preferably just after weaning, in order to be suitable pets. This would mean purchasing an animal that is only five to six weeks old. Other breeders recommend that hedgehogs be between eight and twelve weeks of age before going to a new home. The most rewarding choice may be an adolescent or adult hedgehog with a good, outgoing temperament. These older animals are preferable to the weanling that stays rolled in a tight ball most of the time.

QUICK HEALTH CHECKLIST:

Eyes—clear, bright, injury free

Nose—dry, free of discharge

Ears—erect, clean

Fur—soft, good condition

Rectal/Genital areas—clean, free of moisture and fecal material

Pads on feet—firm, not calloused

Adaptability

One advantage to purchasing a younger hedgehog is that it will usually adapt faster to your family routine than will an adult hedgehog. Hedgehogs are considered to be adolescents from three to six months of age and adults at six months of age. However, an adult hedgehog that has never been tamed will be the most difficult to work with and is not a suitable pet for a first-time hedgehog owner. Ultimately, it should be the individual animal's personality that helps you make your purchase decision.

Bringing Your Hedgehog Home

When you bring your hedgehog home, place it in its cage and give it twenty-four hours to adjust to its new surroundings. This helps lessen the stress of a move to a new home. Carefully observe the amount of food and water consumed by your new pet. If you are using a water bottle, and your pet does not start drinking within twenty-four hours, give it a shallow bowl of water. Use bottled water because tap or well water can have unpleasant tastes or smells. Most hedgehogs will start eating only after they have started drinking in their new home.

Carry on your normal activities in the room where you have placed your hedgehog's cage. It will help it begin to become accustomed to your normal household activity.

HANDLING YOUR HEDGEHOG

When you handle your potential pet, scoop him up gently from underneath along his sides. This helps ensure that you contact fur rather than quills. Sometimes, new owners find it helpful to wear lightweight gloves until they are used to the scooping technique. Give the hedgehog a chance to relax and sniff you. It often helps to gently set the hedgehog on your forearm for support. Outgoing hedgehogs will begin to explore you within the first minute, but shy hedgehogs may never move. If at all possible, handle more than one hedgehog before making your purchase decision.

The average hedgehog accepts handling, but does not come looking for attention. This is the hedgehog that may be easier for a small child to hang on to as it will not be as active when held. This type of hedgehog will be more likely to curl up in the crook of your elbow when comfortable, rather than attempt to climb on to your shoulders and become tangled in your hair. It will appreciate a gentle scratch and a chance to stretch its legs outside its cage, but will probably not actively seek attention. Hedgehogs that are less accepting of human handling or that have been mistreated will stay in a ball for hours without relaxing. These hedgehogs are best left for experienced hedgehog owners or individuals who have experience working with shy or frightened animals.

> ### TREATS FOR THE FINICKY EATER
>
> Treats you can try are meal worms, cooked hamburger, cooked poultry, chopped eggs (hard-cooked or scrambled), cottage cheese (not more than 1 teaspoon), or canned cat or dog foods. Chicken and turkey flavors tend to be the favorite canned foods. You can also try 1 tablespoon of canned or homemade chicken broth in a small bowl or saucer.

WEIGHING IN

Weigh your hedgehog as soon after you purchase him as possible. A postage scale or kitchen scale is ideal.

Kitchen scales offer an advantage over postage scales in that they usually show weights in grams as well as ounces. If your hedgehog ever needs medication, the amount of the dose is determined by its weight in grams. After the initial weigh-in, you should continue to weigh your pet at least once each month and to record the weight. Rapid changes in weight may indicate an underlying health problem.

New Pet Emergencies

One of the most important questions you need to ask is about the current diet of the hedgehog you are thinking about buying. It is always a good idea to maintain the same diet during the initial move from the breeder or pet store to your home. The move may stress the hedgehog, especially if it is from a pet store where it may have gone through two or three moves already.

There are a few common "emergencies" encountered by new hedgehog owners. The first is the refusal of a new pet to eat or drink. Sometimes, due to differences in the taste of water from one community to another, or a change in the type of water bottle, a hedgehog will refuse to drink. If a hedgehog doesn't drink, it usually will not eat either. If your hedgehog does not drink in the first twenty-four to thirty-six hours, provide a shallow saucer or ceramic bowl of water next to the water bottle. If the taste or smell of chlorine or other chemicals is the problem, the saucer will allow the odors to dissipate and the open water will be more acceptable to a hedgehog that is not trained on a water bottle. You can use bottled water to avoid bad tastes or smells. Once you get a hedgehog to drink, it will usually start to eat shortly thereafter.

REFUSAL OF FOOD

If your hedgehog still fails to eat, contact the store or breeder from whom you purchased your pet. Try to feed the same brand of food as it was getting previously. Count or measure the kibble so that you

35

have an accurate picture of the hedgehog's actual food consumption. Normal hedgehogs may consume anywhere from $1/2$ to 2 tablespoons of food per night depending on their appetite, age, activity level and metabolism. Offer the hedgehog's favorite treat foods to see if it will eat anything at all. Try offering several tiny servings suggested in the "Treats for the Finicky Eater" sidebar on a paper plate or saucer. If your hedgehog is active and the stools are a normal, semi-moist consistency, your hedgehog is probably all right and just getting used to its new surroundings. If the hedgehog seems lethargic or depressed, or if the stools are forest green and slimy and do not firm up in twenty-four hours on dry food and water only, something may be wrong, and it is time to take your animal to a veterinarian.

If your new hedgehog is not eating well when you first bring it home, provide it with a variety of small treats as well as time to adjust to its surroundings.

UNEXPECTED PREGNANCY

The new owner of a female hedgehog may encounter an unexpected pregnancy for up to thirty-five days after bringing the hedgehog home. The most important rule is to disturb the new mother as little as possible. Hedgehog moms that are disturbed may kill and eat some or all of their young.

If you discover that your new pet has had babies, first make sure that it has some type of nest box or tube in which to hide. If the babies are scattered, use a spoon to gently scoop them up and place them near their mother. For the first ten days after the babies are born, do little more than replace food and water in the cage.

36

Allow the hedgehog mom to have as much food as it wants to eat. Producing milk for babies consumes a huge quantity of calories. You can use a scoop to clean the litter pan if you can do so quietly without disturbing the nest. Resist the urge to see and handle the babies unless the mother is out of the nest at the time.

A small amount of blood may be passed with the first two or three bowel movements after a mother gives birth and is not a cause for concern. Pools of blood or an extended period of bleeding is a sign that something is wrong, and you should take mom and babies to a qualified veterinarian.

Abandoned Babies

If your hedgehog mom abandons its babies and you decide to hand rear them, goat's milk or a commercial milk replacement in an eye dropper or feeding syringe may be used to feed the babies. Bottle fed babies need to be manually stimulated to produce urine and stool. You can do this by gently stroking the babies near

This hoglet is under three weeks old and has not yet opened its eyes for the first time.

their anal area with a warm, damp cotton ball or large Q-tip. Extra warmth is essential, and is easily provided by placing a heating pad put on a low setting under one end of the cage. This allows the babies the choice of moving to warmer or cooler areas of the cage as their comfort requires.

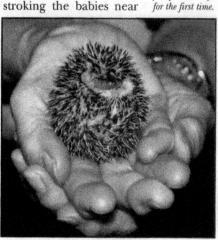

At about three weeks of age the babies' eyes will open and they will become more active. At this point, meat-based baby food or canned or dried kitten food diluted with chicken broth may be added to the feeding routine. Baby hedgehogs are normally weaned at five to six weeks of age.

Living
with a

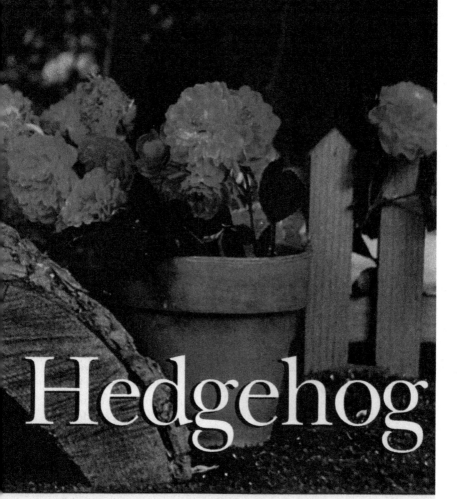

Hedgehog

Bringing Your
Hedgehog
Home

Once you have decided to purchase a hedgehog and have checked to make sure there are no legal restrictions (see chapter 11 for details), the next step is to prepare a home for your pet. It is best to do this prior to bringing your new hedgehog home. This will help the two of you make the best possible start. Purchasing a pet on impulse, then having to provide makeshift accommodations, can expose the pet and yourself to unnecessary stress.

Choosing a Cage

The first decision to make is what type and size of cage to purchase or build. The hedgehog will spend most of its life in a cage, and the size and contents of this cage will influence the health and well-being of your pet.

Since hedgehogs are a relatively new pet, you will not find a commercially designed home specifically for the hedgehog. There are, however, a variety of commercial cages suitable for this small pet. Cages should be at least 18 by 24 inches and cages that are at least 4 square feet in size are preferred. Cages with plastic or metal trays and wire tops are the easiest to clean and disinfect. There are also several nice Plexiglas hedgehog cages available in some pet stores.

Don't forget to lay a protective surface down in a wire cage to protect the hedgehog's feet. Linoleum flooring, shown here, is a good option.

Dwarf rabbit cages 18 inches wide by 24 inches long and 15 inches tall or larger with 6-inch deep solid trays work well for sleeping quarters for hedgehogs. The depth of the tray helps to keep the bedding in the cage when the hedgehog is on its nocturnal rounds. These cages are easily cleaned with lots of ventilation and are available at most pet supply stores and in some discount store pet departments. Small pet cages constructed of 1 inch by 2 inches vinyl coated wire set around or in metal or plastic trays are also appropriate. Please be sure that the cage for your hedgehog has a solid floor. A cage with a mesh bottom is uncomfortable for their small feet which slip through the holes in the wire, and a mesh floor will allow some or all of the bedding to fall through the holes.

41

HOMEMADE CAGES

Whatever variety of cage you choose, select the largest cage that you can fit into your available space. You can also build a cage for your pet. In selecting or constructing a cage, make sure that all materials are glass, Plexiglas, wire, metal, or rigid plastic. Soft plastics and wood will be hard to clean and sanitize properly. When using wire, particularly a hardware type, check to make sure that it is NOT coated with zinc or lead that might be harmful for your pet. Any paint used must be non-toxic and lead-free. If you have the room, plastic tubs for mixing concrete available from your building supply store can be turned into attractive hedgehog playpens or habitats. Several inventive hedgehog owners have constructed wonderful Plexiglas towers or domes for their pets and some of these designs are now being marketed on a small scale.

An aquarium tank with plenty of space for activity is another housing option for the hedgehog.

GETTING CREATIVE

If your space is limited, you can increase the floor area of your hedgehog's quarters by making it a two story home. Two levels can be connected by a ramp to allow the pet to move from one level to another.

You can design decorative living quarters for your hedgehog that are limited only by your imagination. Habitats have been designed with garden, outer space, and landscape themes using old toys, natural and artificial plants, landscaping rocks and other materials. Just be sure that it is safe for your hedgehog as well being an attractive addition to your home.

42

Cage Considerations

PLACEMENT OF THE CAGE

There are a few things to take into consideration when selecting a location for the cage. First, it must be in a draft free area, away from the direct path of open windows, heating vents or air conditioners. Second, do not place the cage in direct sunlight where the hedgehog might get too warm if confined. Hedgehogs in direct sunlight can suffer fatal heatstroke.

LIGHT REQUIREMENTS

It is essential to provide your hedgehog with normal periods of daylight and darkness. Some owners think that if they keep their pets in a dimly lit room that it will encourage activity. However, hedgehogs in the wild hibernate in winter when it is colder and there is less light. Low light levels in captivity decrease rather than increase their activity levels. You should arrange to provide ten to twelve hours of light during winter months to encourage your hedgehog to remain active.

TEMPERATURE

Hedgehogs prefer temperatures of 75 to 80 degrees Fahrenheit with relatively low humidity. They will do well in homes with daytime temperatures between 70 and 90 degrees. Lower temperatures will result in sluggish activity and higher temperatures will cause the hedgehog to stretch out flat and lay panting outside its nest box. In the winter, make sure you keep your cage away from exterior walls that may be colder than the internal room temperature. Pet hedgehogs should NOT be allowed to hibernate as it may prove fatal to the pet. Aestivation, reduced activity during hot weather, is also stressful for pets and excessive heat can result in heat stroke. Pay careful attention to your pet

> **COOLING DOWN IN HOT WEATHER**
>
> If you do not have air-conditioning in your home, it is important to monitor the temperature of your hedgehog's cage. You can freeze water in a plastic milk container and put it in the cage as an "air conditioner" during hot weather if the indoor temperature rises above 90 degrees Fahrenheit.

43

during the warm summer months if you do not have
air-conditioning in your home.

STIMULUS

Hedgehogs can adjust to busy homes, but excessive
noise and its inherent vibrations near the cage will be
stressful for the pet. The important thing to keep in
mind is the fact that hedgehogs need attention and
mental stimulus every day. This includes playtime outside of the cage, toys, a variety of treats and being handled and talked to just like another member of the
family.

Cage Furniture

PELLETS

Bedding for hedgehogs can be any soft, absorbent
material. Suitable bedding include commercial small

*Get creative when
you set up a cage!
Here is a spacious
multilevel cage
with ramps.*

pet bedding made from recycled
paper or paper by-products, and pelleted grass, hardwood chips or aspen
shavings. In a pinch, even shredded
newspaper can be used for bedding.
The pelleted products are generally
the most absorbent and least likely to
lead to wet spots in the cage and
inflammation of the skin. The bedding should be at least 3 inches deep
to satisfy the hedgehog's natural burrowing behavior.

Pelleted bedding has the additional
advantage of being heavy in weight.
This makes it more difficult for the hedgehog to
kick the bedding out of the cage as it burrows and
plays. Also, some pelleted bedding products are able
to be flushed in small quantities and all of them are
compostable.

Shavings

Pine and cedar shavings are frequently used in
hedgehog cages, but are not recommended because

44

wet shavings can result in inflammation of the skin, especially in male hedgehogs. In addition, pine and cedar shavings should never be used due to the high concentration of aromatic oils (which gives them their characteristic odor) that may be irritating to the hedgehog's respiratory system and liver. The use of these shavings has been shown scientifically to cause respiratory irritation and elevation in serum liver enzyme levels in other species, such as rabbits and rodents. Human members of the household may also exhibit respiratory irritation when these products are used.

THE LITTER BOX

If there is room in the cage, supply a small litter pan for your pet. Metal pans 6 inches by 9 inches by 2 inches deep can be obtained from larger pet supply stores and mail-order catalogs. An alternative is to use a plastic drawer divider of similar dimensions, or a terra-cotta tray. Pelleted litters made of plant material or recycled newsprint are preferred as they do not stick to the hedgehog. These have the advantage of being biodegradable after use. Never use the clumping or clay type kitty litter as it will stick to any damp areas on the skin as well as to the eyes, nose and mouth. If you have a male hedgehog and use clay litter, you must check the male daily to make sure that there is no litter stuck to its penis. Damp clay litter or clumping litters can also stick to the anus of both male and female

These are some of the supplies to consider buying for your pet hedgehog, including an exercise wheel, litter box, water bottle, food bowl, nail clippers and toothbrush.

hedgehogs, creating dangerous impactions. Hedgehogs will almost always roll in a freshly cleaned litter pan. This is of little consequence if you are using a pelleted litter, but the dust from a clay litter dehydrates the skin as the dust clings to it. A tablespoon of baking soda may be added to aid in odor control. Place the litter pan as far away from the food dish and water bottle as possible.

Training

Most hedgehogs are naturally neat and will usually defecate and urinate in one area of their cage, even if

they do not have a litter pan. If your hedgehog is not litter box trained, place the litter box in the area of the cage most often used as a bathroom. Clean the rest of the cage, but save a little of the soiled bedding and stool to add to the litter box. This helps direct your hedgehog to the litter pan. If you have more than one hedgehog and one does not understand the purpose of the litter box, put some stool from another hedgehog into the litter box. Male hedgehogs in particular will attempt to cover the scent of their rival with their own excrement.

With patience and persistence hedgehogs can be trained to use a litter box. The box should be placed as far away from the food and water as possible.

Litter Cleaning

Once your hedgehog is used to the litter box, make sure that you keep it clean. Pick out any soiled material daily with a slotted spoon or litter scoop. Empty, wash and refill the litter pan weekly. This will help ensure that there are no unpleasant odors, as well. If you allow the litter pan to become filled with wet litter and excrement, your hedgehog will probably abandon it.

FOOD AND WATER DISHES

You will need two dishes for your hedgehog, one for dry food and one for moist food, and a water bottle or water dish. Small ceramic or earthenware dishes work well as they are harder for the hedgehog to tip over. Dishes that attach to the side of the cage will also help keep the hedgehog from spilling the contents. Placing the dishes on a thin piece of stone, such as a patio stone or brick, will help elevate it a little higher than the bedding.

Snacks can be served in small ceramic bowls and plates. Offer a nutritious variety, such as cut apple, cottage cheese and water, as well as canned and dry cat food.

The Water Bottle

Most hedgehogs will learn to use a hamster or guinea pig water bottle hung on the side of the cage. This allows you to keep water available without constantly cleaning bedding out of a dish. Hang the bottles within reach but above the bedding. A bottle that touches the bedding results in wet bedding and a thirsty hedgehog. Fill the water bottles daily and be careful to check the tips to make sure water is not obstructed and that it is not leaking. Occasionally, a bottle will not release water due to air bubbles, wear or manufacturing defects in the tube or on the bearings. Tap the bottom of the bottle to make sure a drop of water is present on the tip. A newly arrived hedgehog should have water in a dish as well as a bottle in case it does not know how to drink out of a tube.

Your hedgehog will probably learn to climb up the water bottle or water bottle holder. Your cage should have a secure top to prevent your pet from escaping via this makeshift ladder.

If you choose to use a dish, try elevating it above the bedding on a stone or brick just as you would the food dish. Ceramic, wide bottom plastic dishes or weighted bowls work best. Never use a water dish if there are baby hedgehogs in the cage. They can easily drown if they crawl into a deep container of water.

SLEEPING QUARTERS

In the wild, hedgehogs take advantage of whatever cover they can in order to provide a safe sleeping site during the day. This may be under a pile of leaves or brush, in a shallow burrow, in a termite mound, in a rock crevice or under a shed in areas inhabited by humans. All hedgehogs need a place to hide and feel secure while sleeping, so it is important that you add a nest box to your hedgehog's home.

BEDDING MATERIALS

Consider the following items on your list when you shop for your hedgehog's bedding:

- commercial small pet bedding made from recycled paper

- paper by-products

- pelleted grass

- hardwood chips or aspen shavings

- shredded newspaper

This can be a plastic box with a hole cut in one end, a flowerpot turned on its side, a piece of PVC pipe 4 inches in diameter and about 10 inches long, or one of the tunnels sold for small pets. You can even use an old cowboy boot or other decorative object as long as it is easy to clean. For travel or temporary quarters, you can use a cardboard tube or giant size plastic cup. If you purchase a nest box or log at your pet store, make sure that it is of suitable size for an adult hedgehog. Hedgehogs enter and leave their burrows head first, so the opening must be large enough to accommodate an adult hedgehog and the interior roomy enough to allow the animal to turn around.

Offer your hedgehog some soft bedding for the sleeping area. Any of the softer bedding materials, such as wood fibers or aspen shavings are acceptable. Hay, straw and grass can be used as nest material if humans in your household do not have allergies. Some owners offer their hedgehogs pieces of old baby

blankets. These will be dragged, pushed and puffed as
the hedgehog prepares to sleep. You can wash this
"blanket" from time to time to keep it sanitary. Do not
use terry cloth towels as the loops of string are dangerous. Hedgehogs can easily become entangled in the
loose threads when they catch on the quills or claws or
get wrapped around a limb.

EXERCISE WHEELS AND OTHER TOYS

Hedgehogs need exercise to maintain their health
and an easy-going temperament. The most readily
accepted toy is an exercise wheel. Several models specifically designed for hedgehogs are now available. If
they are not available from your local pet store, check
with mail-order sources for small pets such as those
listed in the resource section of this book. Wheels
should be at least 9 inches in diameter and the bars
or mesh must be small enough to prevent the hedgehog from slipping off or between the bars. Solid metal
or plastic wheels provide a better, safer running surface than wire bars or mesh. Wheels designed with a
short spike or bracket to hold the wheel on its stand
rather than a full axle that extends through the wheel
allow more freedom of movement for the hedgehog. It
is normal for hedgehogs to soil their exercise wheel as
they run. Easy to clean plastic needlepoint canvas can
be used to line exercise wheels to aid traction and facil-
itate cleaning.

If you have one of the rare hedgehogs that will not use
an exercise wheel, make sure that your pet has some
exercise time in a closed room, such as a bathroom,
where it can enjoy running and rummaging about
without getting into trouble. Close the cabinet doors
and check carefully that there are no hedgehog-size
openings in the base of the cabinets for him to crawl
into. A playpen may also provide suitable exercise;
these are discussed later in this chapter.

In addition to exercise wheels, hedgehogs may utilize a
variety of other toys. Many hedgehogs will push balls
around their cage or play area. The small balls containing bells sold for cats and ferrets are especially

appealing choices for hedgehogs. Some hedgehogs enjoy pushing plastic sandbox toys around, particularly rolling toys such as trucks. Many hedgehogs will flip the toys over with their nose, then pile them up in one area of the playpen. Small rubber squeaky toys may also be used with hedgehogs.

Hedgehogs enjoy crawling through tunnels of any kind. Tunnels can be created with non-perforated PVC or drainage pipe, old mailing tubes, boxes or bags with holes cut in the ends, or with commercially available tubes and balls labeled for hedgehogs. When purchasing tubes and balls at your pet store, it is important to select only those labeled for hedgehogs or ferrets. The tubes and balls commonly available for hamsters and gerbils are too small for most hedgehogs and can be dangerous to use in a hedgehog cage or play area.

Some hedgehogs like to push toy trucks around.

Mazes and Climbing

Old building blocks can be used to create mazes. You can teach your hedgehog to follow patterns or colors with rewards of its favorite treat. Be patient when attempting this type of training. Hedgehogs do not learn as fast as an average dog.

Hedgehogs love to climb and you can provide cinder blocks, bricks and branches with rough bark in the cage or play area. Just make sure that these are

50

arranged so that the hedgehog cannot get hurt if it topples them.

Playpens

Often, a hedgehog cage is roomy enough for sleeping quarters but not for active play. Remember that in the wild, the hedgehog travels an area up to 1,000 feet in diameter each night as it searches for food. As a hedgehog owner, you will want to make sure that your pet has additional room available for play. This is easily and inexpensively accomplished.

THE TUB

The simplest playpen is a bathtub. Close the drain, then add a layer of newspaper on the bottom of the tub to make cleanup easier. Place a few toys in the tub— your hedgehog's exercise wheel, a ball, some old boxes or bags or even some crumpled newsprint. Add the hedgehog, turn off the lights to simulate evening and wait for the sounds of your pet at play. Do not be disappointed if your hedgehog huddles in one spot the first time or two. Hedgehogs kept in small aquariums or cages sometimes take time to get used to larger quarters and more freedom.

WADING POOL

If the bathtub in your house is not available, try a concrete mixing tub from your local building supply store or an inexpensive children's wading pool. These plastic tubs and pools are easy to clean and the toys you offer in addition to an exercise wheel can be changed periodically to provide some variety for your pet.

Hedgehog Housekeeping

Hedgehogs are most active at night, so it is easiest to clean the litter pan or cage during the day. In the morning, remove the dish used for moist food and wash it. Use a slotted spoon or litter scoop to remove any fecal material and wet areas from the litter pan. Check the bedding for any fecal material, especially underneath or near the exercise wheel. Remove and wash the exercise wheel when it becomes soiled. Check the water bottle daily and refill with fresh water when the bottle is half full. Be especially diligent about checking the water in the summer and with lactating mothers.

MAKING TIME

Your cleaning schedule for your hedgehog will be determined by the size of your cage and the cleanliness of the individual animal. In cages with a single, very neat hedgehog you can wash the cage and replace all the bedding monthly. In cages with several hedgehogs or a single, messy hedgehog, you may need to replace the bedding and wash the cage weekly. Litter pans should be washed and refilled weekly to prevent urine odors from accumulating. A diluted bleach solution or citrus based cleaner is the most appropriate disinfectant.

LITTER CONCERNS

There are several health considerations to look out for regarding the hedgehog's litter use. Litter will stick to any damp areas on the skin as well as to the eyes, nose and mouth; therefore, never use the clumping or clay type of kitty litter. If you choose to use clay litter, you must check the male daily to make sure that there is no litter stuck to its penis. Male and female hedgehogs can suffer from dangerous anal impactions as a result of damp clay litter or clumping litter that sticks to the anus. Check these areas on a regular basis for any problems.

SMELL CONTROL

Hedgehogs are relatively odor free if you keep their cage and litter box clean. However, feeding most canned cat foods and some canned dog foods results in increased odor from the hedgehog droppings. You can tell what had been fed the previous night by the odor. Some of these foods result in moist or slimy fecal material as well—instead of the firm, semimoist droppings normally produced. Some experimenting will help to determine foods that were palatable to the hedgehogs without producing excessive odor.

House Hedgehogs

Some hedgehog owners choose to let their pets roam freely around their homes, or in certain rooms in their homes. Many hedgehogs thrive on this freedom, but during the crucial first weeks in a new home it is important to restrict your hedgehog's movements until it is comfortable in your presence. This allows you to make sure that it is eating and drinking satisfactorily and also to begin the bonding process that is crucial to the success of your hedgehog as a pet. After your pet has settled in, you may gradually increase the amount of freedom you provide.

TAKING PRECAUTIONS

Always keep in mind possible hazards. I discovered after four years of hedgehog ownership that there was a gap in the base of my kitchen cabinets large enough for small hedgehogs to climb in. I almost lost Crystal, one of my favorite cream hedgehogs. My husband was not pleased about the prospect of taking apart the kitchen to retrieve a hedgehog. Hedgehog escapees have found hiding places in our utility room under cabinets, in the legs of our dining room cabinet and one hedgehog mom escaped the night its babies were due and had them under a bookcase. So far, I have retrieved every lost hedgehog, but not without a significant expenditure of time and stress.

Watch the family dog closely when around your pet hedgehog; leaving these two alone together could be hazardous to the hedgehog.

HEDGEHOGS AND OTHER PETS

Although dogs and cats are natural predators, if brought up with hedgehogs, most quickly learn to get

53

along. The spines of a hedgehog are ample protection from an inquisitive dog or cat. Eventually, the hedgehog may become just another pet moving around the home, and some dogs and cats will even share their dinner bowl with the family hedgehog.

It is important, however, during the first few weeks after you bring a hedgehog home to protect it from both direct and indirect attack by other pets. Keep your hedgehog in a secure cage unless both the hedgehog and your other pets are closely supervised. **Dogs** may attempt to pick up the hedgehog and carry it around like a ball or paw at it. Even a small dog could injure or kill a hedgehog with repeated pawing.

Introducing your pet hedgehog to the family cat may help both animals adjust smoothly to living in the same home.

Cats that are good mousers may attack a hedgehog, although house cats are most likely to stress a hedgehog with constant staring. Cats tend to plant themselves next to the hedgehog's cage and stare at it for hours. Once your hedgehog is familiar with the cat, it will probably ignore this behavior. But it may be stressful to a hedgehog that has not yet adjusted to your family members and household routine.

Ferrets are more adept at getting a hold on a hedgehog. Although ferrets and hedgehogs share many households, ferret owners should be cautious about providing their hedgehogs with exercise outside the cage unless the ferrets are securely restrained.

Grooming
Your
Hedgehog

You are probably thinking, how in the world does someone groom a hedgehog? It's actually fairly simple. These little animals with their glossy quills are usually fastidious about their personal hygiene. A hedgehog will require only minimal grooming if you keep its cage clean. When you do need to groom a hedgehog, you will need

an old toothbrush, towels, warm water, a pair of nail clippers, tweezers, a styptic pencil or powder and an emery board or file.

Clipping the Toenails

The hedgehog's toenails grow continuously throughout its life, just like your own nails. In the wild, digging and wear from the ground keeps the nails short and filed. In captivity, especially in a glass or plastic home with soft bedding, there is very little wear on the nails, and they need to be clipped occasionally. It is a good idea to check the nails once a month when you weigh your hedgehog.

First, select a pair of sharp nail clippers or scissors. It is best to reserve a pair specifically for your hedgehog. You can use nail scissors or clippers designed for human nails, and several types of clippers and scissors designed for use on dogs and cats. It is best to select the style that you find the most comfortable and easiest to use.

These are some of the grooming tools for your hedgehog, including a toothbrush, nail file and nail clippers.

If your hedgehog has dirty feet, clean them gently in warm water or with a damp washcloth so that you can see the nail clearly. Work under good lighting, such as near a window during daylight or under a strong incandescent lamp. If you look closely, you should be able to distinguish the point at which the nail grows away from the skin. The nail is white or clear at this point. Where the nail is firmly attached to the skin and has a pinkish color underneath is called the "quick." The quick is where the growing nail is supplied with blood. You want to avoid cutting into this area. Gently but firmly restrain your hedgehog. This is easiest to do if you have someone hold the hedgehog while you gently pull out one leg at a time.

One favorite technique for clipping rear toenails is to run your hands under the hedgehog, then to hold on to the rear legs. Release one leg, then turn the foot on the restrained leg gently backward or to the side. This allows you to see the nails. Clip the tips of any long nails. Hedgehogs tend to wear their nails unevenly—you may have to clip only one or two long nails, usually those on the inside of the foot. If you clip too short and get some bleeding, apply the styptic pencil or powder to the nail and wait for the bleeding to stop before proceeding.

If your hedgehog struggles vigorously, you may want to do one foot per session rather than attempting to clip all four sets of nails at once. If your hedgehog remains relaxed, proceed with the next foot. The front feet of most hedgehogs need less trimming than the back feet. This is a good thing, because trimming the front feet is a little more challenging. The nails are smaller and sharper, and tend to grow in an inward curved manner.

Before you bathe your hedgehog, make sure that the quills are free of any debris. Use of tweezers is helpful for removing especially small particles.

CLIPPING TIPS

If you are right-handed, hold your hedgehog with your left hand to trim the nails on the front feet. Let the rear legs rest on the table or your lap. Use your right hand to gently pull the right leg forward and slightly to the right side of the body. Now transfer the hold on the leg to your left hand, supporting the front end of the hedgehog against your wrist, slightly off the table. Carefully clip the front nails. These nails are usually smaller than the back nails and seldom need to be filed. Release the right leg. Use your right hand to gently pull the left leg forward and slightly to the left side of the body. Again, support the hedgehog against your left wrist with the front end slightly off the table if necessary and the leg held in your left hand. Clip the nails carefully, then gently release your hedgehog. Reverse the holds if you are left-handed.

Another technique for clipping front nails is to roll your hedgehog into a ball and place it on its back. Allow it to unroll slightly. As the hedgehog unrolls it will usually extend the front legs as it attempts to turn over. Gently grasp and hold a front leg as you clip the nails. This technique is sometimes useful for trimming toenails on the back feet—however it is easier for the hedgehog to keep its back legs tucked under the folds of skin when in this position.

Be gentle when restraining your hedgehog, but keep a firm grasp of the leg while clipping the toenails.

ALTERNATIVES TO CLIPPING

If you would like to try to avoid clipping nails, provide the hedgehog with some type of rough surface to play on in its cage or playpen to help keep the nails worn down. Suitable items include aquarium rocks, bricks or patio blocks. Place these in such a way that the hedgehog walks on them—but be careful that they cannot fall over and crush the hedgehog. Some pet owners place the food and water dishes on a patio stone or pair of bricks. This not only encourages the hedgehog to walk on the rough surface, but elevates the food dish and helps keep it clean.

The Bath

Now that you have clipped the nails, it's time for a grooming or a bath. First, use the tweezers to remove any bedding or other material lodged between the quills. Regular grooming of the quills is done by placing the hedgehog on a towel on the table or in your lap. Dip a toothbrush in warm water and gently stroke the quills from front to back. Rinse the toothbrush frequently as you move from one area of quills to another. If your hedgehog enjoys the attention, you can also use the toothbrush on the fur areas. If your hedgehog is one of those who enjoys grooming, use a dry toothbrush to brush its quills and fur on a regular basis as part of your handling routine.

If your hedgehog is really dirty, has been anointing a lot or rolling in its litter pan, you will want to try a bath or shower. A bath can also be soothing to a hedgehog that is recovering from an external parasite infestation. Close the drain in your kitchen sink, cover the bottom of the sink with an old towel and place your hedgehog on the towel. If you have a vegetable sprayer attachment on the sink, gently spray the hedgehog with lukewarm water. If you do not have a sprayer, use a cup to gently pour warm water over your pet. Avoid getting water or spray in the hedgehog's eyes and nose. You can let up to one-half inch of water accumulate in the sink to help wash the legs and belly.

Once the hedgehog is thoroughly wet, use a wet toothbrush to remove any dirt and debris from the quills by brushing gently from front to back, rinsing the toothbrush often. When you have finished brushing the quills, gently rinse the hedgehog with

> **ESSENTIAL GROOMING TOOLS**
>
> old toothbrush
>
> several towels (not terry cloth)
>
> warm water
>
> pair of nail clippers
>
> tweezers
>
> styptic pencil or powder
>
> emery board or file

plenty of plain, lukewarm water from the sprayer or from a cup.

DRYING OFF

Wrap the hedgehog in a towel to remove as much water as possible. Switch to a dry towel and hold your animal in your lap, stroking him with a dry

area of the towel, until thoroughly dry. Be cautious about putting your hedgehog back in the cage before it is fully dry, especially in the winter. Some types of bedding will stick to a damp hedgehog, defeating the grooming and causing the hedgehog to be uncomfortable.

DUST BATH

There is one more item that should be mentioned in re-

After your hedgehog is used to being groomed, a warm bath may be necessary for cleaning or soothing irritated skin. The kitchen sink and a light spray or cup of water will work well to wet the hedgehog.

gard to grooming and that is the dust bath. Although none of the hedgehog literature suggests that they routinely take dust baths in the wild, many captive-raised hedgehogs enjoy taking dust baths in any material that suits them. Be cautious if your hedgehog takes a dust bath. There is a potential risk of eye injuries, of material inhaled up the nose or material sticking to the genital area and causing impaction as well as infection.

Other Grooming Essentials

TEETH

Older hedgehogs should have their teeth checked periodically for tooth and gum disease, also called peridontia. Providing hedgehogs with dry cat food as the major part of their diet will help to keep tartar from building up on the teeth and reduce the likelihood of dental problems, but it doesn't prevent tartar or gum disease entirely.

EARS

Hedgehog ears should be soft, with smooth edges. If your hedgehog develops ragged ear edges, it should be examined by a veterinarian. Rough, dry ear edges can be caused by external parasites, fungal infections or excessively dry skin.

SKIN CARE

Dry skin may be treated by adding a few drops of vegetable oil or a fatty acid supplement to the dry cat food every day. Take care to monitor your hedgehog's weight when adding oil to its diet. If too much oil is used it can

Some hedgehogs love to take a dust bath.

cause a rapid increase in body weight. In addition to oil in the diet, your veterinarian can suggest products that are safe to use on your hedgehog to improve the skin quality.

EYES

Hedgehog eyes should be clear, bright and moist. Dull eyes, cloudy spots in the eyes, excessive tearing and scratching at the eye area are all indications that something is wrong. Eyes are not something that should be treated by a pet owner without veterinary supervision. A hedgehog that scratches at the eye area can easily injure the eye. If your hedgehog develops an eye problem or injures an eye, take it to your veterinarian for diagnosis and treatment.

> **SIGNS OF A HEALTHY HEDGEHOG:**
>
> Bright, clear eyes
>
> Clean skin, free of flakes
>
> No dandruff between quills
>
> Ears that are soft and smooth
>
> Hearty appetite
>
> Active and inquisitive nature

Hedgehog
Nutrition

Food Sources in the Wild

In the wild, hedgehogs are opportunistic feeders. Although classed as insectivores, they are omnivorous, meaning they will eat foods of both animal and plant origin. Even though they may have preferences, they will eat whatever is handy, plentiful or easy to catch. In fact, many of the hedgehogs imported into the United States were trapped in their native Africa around garbage dumps where they could be caught foraging at night. Research indicates that the various hedgehog species consume an extremely varied menu, including insects, worms, snails, baby mice and other tiny mammals. Evidence has also been found that at times they consume small crabs, lizards, snakes, broken eggs, carrion, various fruits, roots, fungi, small fish and frogs. Of course, not every hedgehog will eat all of this, and some hedgehogs are extremely selective in their choice of food.

A Basic Hedgehog Diet for Your Pet

How do you translate this varied diet into a practical menu for your pet hedgehog? There is still much research that needs to be done on the nutritional requirements of the captive hedgehog. Currently, the basis for a good, balanced hedgehog diet starts with dry cat food or dry hedgehog food. It is still difficult to find high quality, commercially prepared hedgehog foods but there are now several low-iron products available through pet stores and catalog sources. Some animal nutritionists now believe that a low-iron diet is the most appropriate for the pet hedgehog.

DRY FOOD

In the absence of hedgehog food, select a good quality dry cat food from your veterinarian or a pet store. Do not use the products in the bulk bins of the grocery store. Try to pick a cat food with meat or poultry listed as the first ingredient and a high protein level. Avoid brands that are fish based or that contain nuts and seeds. The shape of the food is also important to some hedgehogs.

In the wild, the insects eaten by the hedgehog provide a moist and crunchy diet. The dry food substitutes for the crunchy part of the diet. It provides a balanced meal and the hard pellets help to keep tartar from forming on the hedgehog's teeth. It is difficult to clean a hedgehog's teeth without anesthetizing the animal. Hard, dry food is a much more convenient alternative to a tiny hedgehog toothbrush!

Choosing the Formula

The formula of the dry food (growth, maintenance or reduced calorie) should be based on the age, health and activity level of the pet hedgehog. When a prepared hedgehog diet is not available, most breeders feed kitten food to the juvenile hedgehogs just starting to eat solid food and continue this up until about ten weeks of age. At that point, they gradually switch the hedgehog over to a maintenance or reduced calorie formula.

The reduced calorie formula of either cat food or hedgehog food is a good choice for most adult hedgehogs. The exception is nursing mothers who have a high calorie requirement and should be eating the maintenance formula. Once a hedgehog becomes fat in captivity, it usually also becomes sluggish. Overweight hedgehogs have shortened life spans and are more prone to a variety of illnesses including fatty liver disease, heart disease and respiratory disease.

How Much Is Enough?

How much dry food should you feed each day? This is a very difficult question to answer because hedgehogs vary considerably in size and activity levels. Hedgehogs may range in weight from a tiny 11 ounce animal to a long, large 20 ounce animal that is just big, not overweight.

To determine how much to feed, start by weighing your pet at least every two weeks to keep track of weight gain or loss. Postage scales and kitchen scales that measure in small increments of up to 2 or 5 pounds usually work well. The belly of a hedgehog held in your palm should feel flat, neither protruding and soft nor concave and bony.

When you start out with your new hedgehog, weigh it to get a beginning weight. You can also ask the breeder or pet store to do this for you before you bring your animal home. Start by feeding 1 tablespoon of dry food, either cat or hedgehog, every day. Young hedgehogs should gain about 1 ounce of weight per week until they reach twelve weeks of age. At that point, their weight will begin to stabilize. A hedgehog is usually considered mature at six months of age and should cease to gain weight at this point in time.

Adjust the amount of the dry food up or down, depending on the activity level of your pet. Some small hedgehogs eat twice as much as their larger counterparts because they are more active or have a different metabolic rate. Nursing mothers should be offered dry food freely.

Only 1 teaspoon per day of wet food is required for most hedgehogs.

MOIST FOOD

In addition to the dry food, supplement the diet with moist foods such as canned cat or dog food based on meat or poultry, low-fat cottage cheese, cooked eggs and cooked poultry. Alternate these moist foods, giving a total of about one teaspoon per day. The proportion over one week's time is about one-half canned cat or dog food, one-fourth cottage cheese and one-fourth from other protein sources including cooked egg, cooked poultry or occasionally a treat of cooked hamburger. It is important to remember that these items are fed at the rate of *only* 1 teaspoon per day for most hedgehogs.

FRUITS AND VEGGIES

In addition to the moist foods, feed small amounts of fruits and vegetables. Try cooked yams, apples, applesauce, grapes and frozen mixed vegetables, especially peas and corn. Some hedgehog breeders and owners have reported success with greens, melon, banana and carrots. The daily quantity of fruits and vegetables is *very small*. The daily amount translates into a small cube of fruit, half a grape, two kernels of corn or two peas. The amount measures about $1/4$ teaspoon. Do not overfeed fruits and vegetables because hedgehogs are not vegetarians. These items are meant to substitute for what the hedgehog would have consumed by eating the stomachs of its insect or mammal victims. Do not worry too much if your hedgehog refuses fruits and vegetables. Just continue to offer *tiny* bits of whatever you are eating and eventually you may find something your hedgehog enjoys.

> **A NOTE FOR VEGETARIANS**
>
> Please keep in mind that hedgehogs are not natural vegetarians and must have a meat-based diet. You can offer very small bits of treats, but be careful not to overfeed fruits and vegetables. Some items to try include a tiny cube of fruit, half a grape, two peas or a couple kernels of corn.

Water is an essential part of the hedgehog diet. Monitor the water bottle and/or water dish to be sure your pet is properly hydrated.

HYDRATE!

Always make sure your hedgehog has clean, fresh water available. Keep track of both its water and food consumption. Changes in the typical amount of water or food consumed can signal the onset of changes in health. Hedgehogs often do not show signs of illness until they are near death. This is okay in the wild because signs of illness may make a hedgehog more vulnerable to predation. In captivity this stoic behavior is less desirable because it may hide a potentially dangerous health problem. If your hedgehog's eating habits change, look around for any other indicators of ill health, such as lethargy and depression, green stool or cloudy eyes.

This hedgehog has a balanced menu including dry cat food, an apple slice, cottage cheese, water and canned cat food in a separate bowl.

When and How to Feed

The best time to feed hedgehogs is in the evening. Hedgehogs are the most active at night, so the food will arrive when they are normally ready to start foraging. Some pet owners split the feeding, providing the moist food as a treat at the time they plan to play with their pet, then replenishing the dry food later in the evening.

HYGIENE

Provide separate dishes for the dry food and moist foods. If you are feeding in the evening, remove any uneaten moist food the following morning and wash the dishes thoroughly. Uneaten dry food can be left in the cage at all times if the hedgehog has not soiled the food. All foods should be at room temperature.

Provide your pet with a water tube, bottle or dish. Refill small water tubes and dishes daily, and refill larger water bottles when they are half empty. Wash the water bottles or dishes on a regular basis to prevent the formation of mold or algae. Water is a very important part of the hedgehog's diet. If a hedgehog is not drinking, it is also not likely eating.

Treat Foods

If you are not squeamish about feeding live food, most hedgehogs will come running for mealworms, waxworms or crickets. You can feed three to five mealworms, one waxworm or a couple of crickets per day. It is not necessary to kill the worms prior to feeding.

Some pet owners add the mealworms to the dinner dish, others scatter them about the cage so that the hedgehog has to forage for them, much as they would have to in the wild.

A diet composed primarily of mealworms will be high in fat and have low levels of calcium. Use mealworms and other insects as a treat food in the diet, not the entire diet. To increase the nutritional value of the mealworms or crickets, you can feed the mealworms or crickets prior to feeding them to your hedgehogs. This helps the insects to have stomachs full of predigested plant protein when the hedgehogs eat them.

This hedgehog is searching the crevices of a rock for some tasty mealworms to snack on.

Other treat foods that seem to be popular with hedgehogs are cooked hamburger (no ketchup or mustard please!), cooked chicken and other poultry, and chicken broth. Hamburger should be used sparingly as a treat food due to the high fat content. Small bits of poultry fed without the skin are readily eaten by most hedgehogs, as are both homemade and canned chicken broth.

Some hedgehogs also enjoy the semimoist treats sold for cats and dogs. If you can obtain sample packages or buy these for your other household pets, you can try small pieces of the treat with your hedgehog. Some hedgehogs will also chew on thin pieces of rawhide, but some appear to use them more for self-anointing than for any dietary need.

Historically, wild European hedgehogs have been offered bread soaked in milk to attract them to gardens. The hedgehog's stomach is NOT designed to digest cow's milk. If you feed milk as a treat, you will likely discover the next morning that your hedgehog is suffering from diarrhea and that its cage has patches of forest green, liquid stool. Milk is not a recommended treat.

> **GETTING CREATIVE WITH TREATS**
>
> In a playpen, you can place mealworms in the small crevices and depressions of a climbing rock or scatter them on the patio stone used to keep the water and food dishes elevated above the bedding. The hedgehogs climb about the rock searching for their treats. The rough stone helps keep their toenails worn down and the activity of climbing and foraging for treats is a good mental and physical activity for your pets.

Supplements

There is still much controversy over the addition of vitamins to hedgehog diets. Your veterinarian can help you determine whether they are appropriate for your pet. A diet based on a high quality dry food complemented by a variety of moist foods is preferable to reliance on supplements.

Foods to Use with Caution

In the rush to get new hedgehog products on the market, some manufacturers have reformulated or merely relabeled products developed for other small mammals. Unfortunately, some of these diets and treats were developed for rodents that eat a grain and vegetable based diet. Read the package carefully before purchasing the product, and avoid those that have a high grain content.

Do not feed foods containing shelled peanuts. There are cases where hedgehogs required veterinary treatment to remove peanut halves stuck in the roof of their mouths between the teeth.

Keeping Your
Hedgehog
Healthy

by Susan A. Brown, DVM

African hedgehogs are remarkably hearty pets considering the short amount of time they have been maintained in captivity and how much there still is to learn about their captive husbandry requirements. However, you may be faced with a situation where your pet needs medical attention. It is advisable to find a veterinarian who will be willing to treat your unusual pet before an emergency arises.

Finding a Veterinarian

It may be difficult to find a veterinarian in your area who has experience treating hedgehogs. Veterinarians do not learn about them in veterinary school. However, if you can find a veterinarian who is willing to work with you and locate information when he or she doesn't know the answer, this is an important starting point. Give your veterinarian a copy of this book with the additional reference list in the back. You might start your search for a veterinarian by calling the hedgehog groups that are listed in the resources chapter and ask if they have a veterinary referral list. Next ask local hedgehog owners, breeders or pet stores who they would recommend. Finally, make calls to veterinary clinics in your area and ask if they have experience treating hedgehogs or are willing to see your pet. In addition, check to see if the veterinarian you choose will see hedgehogs on an after-hours emergency basis. If after-hours emergencies are referred to an emergency clinic, make sure that clinic will accept hedgehogs. Again, it is better to be prepared than to be left without help when you are in dire need of it.

It is important to take your hedgehog for a health exam when you first purchase it.

It is an excellent idea to have your veterinarian perform a health exam soon after your hedgehog is purchased. In this way you can be protected against any problems you might have missed, you have a chance to meet and become familiar with your veterinarian and your veterinarian can become familiar with your pet.

It is often necessary for a veterinarian to anesthetize a hedgehog in order to examine it thoroughly and to collect blood samples, urine samples or perform X rays or ultrasound. With the use of modern inhalation anesthetics, this is generally a safe procedure and

71

far less stressful than performing diagnostics while the pet is awake.

Once you have established a working relationship with a veterinarian, it is recommended that you have your pet examined at least once a year. As the pet reaches middle age, at around three to four years, it may be advisable to start semiannual veterinary visits to manage the diseases of aging, including cancer and dental disease.

Emergency Care

If you have an emergency with your hedgehog, there are a few things you can do for your pet until you can get to a veterinary clinic. Always transport an ill hedgehog in a small secure container that can be kept warm, particularly in cold climates. If an ill hedgehog becomes chilled, it can lead to serious and potentially fatal complications. A hot water bottle or any of the chemical hand warmers can be placed under a soft towel in the bottom of the container to keep the pet warm. Make sure the lid of the container is perforated for ventilation. When the weather is cold, warm up the car before placing the hedgehog in it.

BLEEDING

If your pet is bleeding, put firm pressure on the area to slow or stop the flow of blood. Apply undiluted hydrogen peroxide, styptic powder, flour or cornstarch to a small wound or bleeding nail to slow or stop the bleeding. Do not use powdered products on large open wounds. It is difficult to keep a bandage on a hedgehog, but if there is a large wound on the body that needs to be covered, gauze or Telfa pads may be held in place by slipping a small section of a sock over the body, from front to back like a tube. The quills will help to keep it in place and it can be easily cut off at the veterinarian's office. If there is bleeding from the nose or mouth, do not apply pressure to the face, but rather keep the hedgehog quiet in a small dark box to minimize movement and get medical attention immediately.

Diarrhea and Vomiting

If your pet is experiencing severe diarrhea or is vomiting, remove all food and offer only small amounts of water. Save samples of vomit or stool in a tightly closed plastic bag so your veterinarian can examine this material. These samples will keep for two to six hours, particularly if they are kept cool. Do not store these samples anywhere near human food supplies. Wash your hands thoroughly after handling your pet. You can check your pet for dehydration by pulling up on a small section of quills over the back, letting go and seeing how quickly the skin returns to its normal place. Normal hedgehog skin will go back into its normal position immediately, whereas dehydrated hedgehog skin will slowly regain its normal position over several seconds. You may offer a warmed pediatric oral electrolyte solution, found in most grocery stores in the baby food section, or a small amount of honey in warm water orally. Using an eyedropper or syringe, hold the hedgehog so that the head is elevated, but the pet is not completely on its back, and slowly push the fluid into the mouth. Give only as much as the hedgehog will take willingly and allow it to swallow before giving more. If your pet vomits within a few minutes discontinue oral fluids immediately. Hedgehogs that are having severe diarrhea or are vomiting need immediate medical attention.

> ### SIGNS OF ILL HEALTH
>
> Animals can't verbally communicate how they feel, so how will you know if your hedgehog is ill? Besides behavioral changes, here are some signs to look out for:
>
> - dull looking eyes
> - lethargy
> - decrease or loss of appetite
> - constipation/diarrhea
> - discharge from eyes or nose
> - labored breathing
> - unexplained weight loss
> - bloated abdomen

Shock

If your hedgehog is weak or is unable to move, it may be in severe shock caused by a variety of conditions (such as heat stroke, liver or kidney failure, septicemia, severe dehydration, intestinal blockage etc.) or may be suffering from a neurological disease or a fractured limb. Handle your pet as little as possible in case there is an injury to the spine and to reduce further stress. Slide the hedgehog onto a piece of firm cardboard or thin wood to transport it to a small box padded with soft towels. Place a heating pad, hot water bottle or chemical hand warmer underneath the towels to provide heat. Get your pet to a veterinarian immediately.

Keep your hedge-hog in a warm environment to avoid hypothermia.

LOW BODY TEMPERATURE

Occasionally a hedgehog that is acting sluggish is simply suffering from hypothermia (low body temperature) due to an environmental temperature that is too low. If you warm up your pet as described previously, it should respond within an hour or two and become much more lively and want to get out of the box. However, if the hedgehog doesn't completely resume its normal activities, it should be taken to a veterinarian to be checked.

Medication Techniques

There is no doubt about it—hedgehogs can be a challenge to medicate! With their ability to roll up into a ball, it can be impossible to give medications by mouth or into the eyes or ears. In addition, a hedgehog may become shy around you if it has an unpleasant experience with medicating. Please refer to Chapter 8, "Socializing Your Hedgehog," for ways of reducing stress when handling your pet for medication.

INJECTIONS

Injectable medications are often preferable to oral medications because they can be given even when the hedgehog is in a ball. In addition, the pet can't see who is giving the medication and you may be spared its shyness later on. Hedgehogs have a large amount

of space under the skin that can accept a variety of

medications plus injectable fluids that might be given if the pet is dehydrated. Hedgehogs tolerate injections fairly well, but may occasionally "pop" or jump when you first try to give the injection. Your veterinarian will show you the proper way to use and dispose of needles, syringes and injectable medications.

ORAL MEDICATIONS

Oral medications are best given by masking them with a pleasant taste and getting the hedgehog to take them on its own. Check with your veterinarian before using any of these products to make sure there is no potential reaction with the medication(s) you are using. Hedgehogs have a sweet tooth and some favorite flavors include chocolate (use imitation chocolate flavoring), banana, vanilla and cherry. In addition some hedgehogs will accept medications if they are mixed with strained meat human baby foods such as chicken or turkey, or canned cat or dog food. Try some of these flavors or experiment with others (with the permission of your veterinarian) without the medication at first, and then when an acceptable taste is discovered, mix one part medication with three parts flavoring and try again. Do not give medications mixed with a whole bowl of the regular diet because you cannot be sure that your pet will get the entire dose, and your pet may reject its food altogether in the future if it doesn't like the medication taste.

> **TECHNIQUES FOR SCRUFF HOLDING**
>
> Use a pair of lightweight latex gloves for better traction when grasping the quills. Grasp the section of skin and quills between and slightly behind the ears while the pet is in a normal standing position. (This method will not work if the pet is already rolled up in a ball.) Lift the hedgehog up off the table so its hind quarters are suspended. Initially your pet will try to roll up into a ball , but it is very difficult to maintain a balled position because the scruff hold is preventing it. Wait until the back legs relax. You will then have access to the mouth, the eyes and the ears.

EYE AND EAR MEDICATIONS

It can be challenging to medicate hedgehog eyes and ears without the scruff hold in the docile hedgehog and impossible if the pet is shy. Ask your veterinarian to provide eye or ear medication in a drop formula rather than in ointment because drops are easier to administer and less messy for the pet. To medicate the ears, wait until the pet is in a normal standing position, get as close to the head as possible without eliciting a defensive reaction and drop the medication directly into the ear canal. If you touch the sensitive facial hairs or ears your pet will pull its quills over its face, and then you will have to wait until it is relaxed again. The same method is used for eye medication, dropping it from above where it is more difficult for the hedgehog to see it coming. Make sure both eye and ear medications are at room temperature before administering them to minimize discomfort to your pet.

MEDICATION DANGERS

When applying medication to skin lesions be aware of two potential dangers. The first danger is that if the

hedgehog licks the medication and swallows it, the drug can be absorbed through the intestinal tract into the body. In very tiny amounts, this may not be a problem, but if you apply large "globs" of material, it could potentially lead to a serious toxicity. Secondly, if the hedgehog really likes the taste of the ointment, it may be so vigorous about

This hedgehog is self-anointing, a normal reaction to the taste and smell of the medication administered.

eating it that it literally mutilates the skin underneath. Watch for signs that the pet is chewing at its skin. If this becomes apparent, notify your veterinarian immediately and wash the medication from the skin. It may be necessary for your veterinarian to change medications or apply a restraint device to prevent the hedgehog from reaching the affected area.

REDUCING STRESS

After each medication, spend some quiet time with your hedgehog. You may notice your pet anointing itself, probably trying to get rid of the taste or smell of the medication. Allow your pet to relax and investigate you and talk to it in quiet tones. If there is a favorite treat food, such as a mealworm, this should be given as a "reward" for being such a good patient. All attempts at making the medication experience as non-stressful as possible will pay off in the end with a pet that doesn't become "medication shy" around you.

Post Mortems

If a pet hedgehog dies, particularly if you or your veterinarian do not know the cause of death, it can be very helpful to have a post mortem examination done. This will, of course, be a personal decision on your part, but consider two very important points. The first is that if you have other hedgehogs in the house, it is important to know what the one in question died of to know if your other pets are at risk. In this way, a post mortem exam can act as a preventative for further disease spread and potential loss of the lives of your other pets. Secondly, there is still so little known about hedgehog disease compared to other pets such as dogs and cats, that the more information that can be gathered on these pets, the better the veterinary community will be able to deal with hedgehog medical problems in the future.

Hedgehog Disease

Most domestic pets have the potential to spread disease to their human companions. Hedgehogs are no exception. Although disease transmission between hedgehog and human is not common, it can potentially happen with such diseases as salmonellosis and external parasites. The best prevention for disease transmission is to use good hygiene around hedgehogs or any other pet for that matter. This means washing your hands thoroughly after handling your pet, particularly before eating. Do not wash hedgehog food and water containers or cages in or near human food preparation areas. If there is anyone in the household who has a weakened immune system, he or she should not be allowed to clean the hedgehog's cage or food and water containers. In addition, children should be instructed in the proper handling of the pet and also should not be allowed to clean the cage until they are old enough to understand the responsibility of hand washing afterwards.

You do not need to be afraid of your hedgehog because the likelihood of picking up a disease from a person you are in contact with is far greater than contracting a disease from your pet. The key disease prevention is common sense and consistent hygienic habits around your hedgehog and other pets.

SKIN DISEASE

Skin disease is one of the most common reasons that pet African hedgehogs need to see a veterinarian.

If your hedgehog looks uncomfortable and is scratching excessively it should be checked for skin disease by the veterinarian.

Normal hedgehog skin should be smooth with occasional small flakes of dried skin. If you notice heavy flaking, quill loss or hair loss, scabs, redness, ragged or crusted ears or swollen, crusted paws there is a problem. In addition, some hedgehogs will be scratching at themselves constantly. The most common skin disease is caused by a microscopic sarcoptid mange mite. This parasite lives and breeds on the skin and can be transmitted from hedgehog to hedgehog by direct contact. Your veterinarian can diagnose the presence of the parasites by examining a small scraping of skin under the microscope for mites and eggs. The condition is treated with an injectable antiparasitic drug. The injection will be repeated two to four times depending on the severity of the disease. All the hedgehogs in the household should be treated because some may be affected and not be showing signs yet. In addition, it will be necessary to clean the bedding and cages thoroughly because the mites can live for brief periods off of the pet. Your veterinarian may recommend that you use a light dusting of a desiccant-type product or a mild insecticide around the cage or under the bedding.

PARASITES

Hedgehogs can be infested with the same fleas and ticks that are found on cats and dogs. A tick should be removed by firmly grasping it as close to its attachment to the skin as possible and pulling it out. The area can be cleaned with a skin disinfectant afterwards. Fleas can be eradicated by using a mild flea shampoo or flea powder that is safe for cats. Avoid getting these products in the hedgehog's eyes, ears, nose or mouth. Since both fleas and ticks breed and lay eggs off the pet in cracks and crevices around floors and walls, it will be necessary to treat the cage and room also, as well as any other pets in the household that might be infested. Your veterinarian can advise you on the proper eradication techniques. Fleas and ticks can carry infectious diseases which can be transmitted through their bites. It is unknown at the time of this writing whether the African hedgehog is susceptible to any of these diseases.

If you keep your pet hedgehog outdoors, it can be exposed to fly larvae. One type of fly, known as *Cuterebra,* lays eggs around the cage door which then adhere to the hedgehog when the hedgehog rubs up against this area. Each egg hatches into a single large larva that burrows into the skin and continues to grow. You will see a large lump forming under the skin with a small hole at its tip, which is the larva breathing hole. These larvae can be safely removed by your veterinarian. There is no aftercare needed once the larva is gone and the hole it occupied is flushed with an antiseptic solution.

Maggots are the larvae of a variety of other species of flies. If your hedgehog becomes soiled with feces it can attract an adult fly which lays its eggs directly on the hedgehog's skin. The larvae hatch out in twenty-four hours and start feeding on the skin immediately. In literally a matter of hours, significant damage can take place. You can remove some of the maggots by washing your pet immediately with copious amounts of warm water and then using hydrogen peroxide on the area and rinsing again. Your pet should be taken to a veterinarian as soon as possible because some maggots may have burrowed deep into the skin. In addition, there may be severe skin damage with the potential for bacterial skin disease to develop.

Hedgehogs can develop fungal disease of the skin ("ringworm") most commonly caused by an organism called *Trichophyton mentagrophytes*. This fungus can also affect cats, dogs and humans. The signs of the disease are similar to those seen with mange mites, but the hedgehog is usually not "itchy." The lesions appear primarily around the face and ears with dry, crusty and scaly skin. A veterinarian can make the diagnosis by plucking some affected hair or quills and performing a fungal culture. The treatment may include both topical and oral medications. It is necessary to treat all the hedgehogs that might have had contact with the infected one. In addition, other household pets should be examined by your veterinarian and may also be treated. Skin lesions on humans may appear as slightly raised red patches. Contact your physician for proper treatment in humans.

Other skin diseases of the hedgehog are bacterial, allergic and neoplastic (cancerous).

EYE PROBLEMS

Hedgehog eye disease is not common, most likely due to the excellent protection the quills provide when they are pulled over the face. Hedgehogs can sustain eye injuries due to fighting or contact with protruding cage wires. These pets can also develop infectious eye disease. Although not reported as of this writing, it is likely that hedgehogs can develop cataracts and glaucoma. A hedgehog's eyes should be clear, bright and dark. If you notice swelling of the lids or of the eye itself, excessive tearing, squinting, staining of the face with eye discharge or a closed eye there is a potentially serious problem that needs immediate medical attention. You can gently clean the eyelids or the area around the eye with warm water or saline on a cotton ball if there is dried discharge that might be causing discomfort. Particularly in the case of eye injuries, it is important to get your pet to a veterinarian as soon as possible in order to try to save the vision.

EAR PROBLEMS

The most common disease that afflicts the ears of the hedgehog is mange mites. The second most common is fungal disease. The normal hedgehog ear appearance is thin, nearly hairless skin with a smooth edge. There should be little or no wax present in the ear canal. The signs of both fungal and parasitic disease are similar and include crusting and thickening of the ear edges, ragged ear edges, flaking of the skin on the ear flap and sometimes accumulation of wax in the ear

An ear examination by the veterinarian will be necessary to diagnose an infection, which you can suspect if your hedgehog is tilting or circling its head.

canal. The treatment for these conditions is found under the section on skin disease earlier in this chapter. In addition, hedgehogs can be infested with the same ear mites that can affect cats, dogs and ferrets. The signs include excessive ear wax and frequent scratching at the ears. The diagnosis is made by either seeing the mites with the naked eye moving about in the ear (they are

white and about the size of the head of a pin) or by examining a sample of wax from the ear under the microscope looking for mites and eggs. The treatment can vary from topical medication to injections of an antiparasitic drug. All animals that are in contact with the affected hedgehog should be treated.

Hedgehogs can also develop bacterial ear infections. The discharge in the ear will be of a more liquid consistency than normal ear wax and will often have a foul smell. In addition, the pet will be sensitive to touch on that side of its face. The diagnosis is made by examining the ear and the discharge. Your veterinarian may wish to perform a bacterial culture on the material in the ear to aid in selecting an antibiotic. Antibiotics are used topically in the ear and in severe infections are also given orally.

If a hedgehog develops an inner ear infection, it may exhibit a head tilt or circle to one side. Damage to the brain can also cause these signs. Get medical attention for your pet as soon as possible.

DENTAL DISEASE OR DENTAL PROBLEMS

Captive African hedgehogs are often afflicted with tooth and gum disease. This may be due to a diet that is insufficiently high in food items that stimulate the gum tissue. Using hard food as a major portion of the diet is the best prevention, but as the pet ages gum and

tooth disease may still develop. Normal hedgehog teeth are white and the gums should be a healthy medium to dark pink in color. Signs of dental disease include a decreased or complete loss of appetite, drooling, a foul odor to the breath, reddened and/or swollen gums, tooth discoloration and pawing at the mouth.

A varied diet, including crunchy food items to stimulate the gum tissue, will help to maintain oral health for your hedgehog's teeth.

These signs indicate a serious problem and you should seek medical attention for your pet right away. Your veterinarian may need to take an X ray to see if there are any tooth root infections prior to instituting treatment. Some hedgehogs who have lost a significant amount of teeth will need to switch over to a soft diet because they have lost the ability to break down hard food.

RESPIRATORY DISEASE

The most common cause of respiratory disease in hedgehogs is bacterial infection. There are a variety of bacteria that can cause problems in these pets including *Bordetella bronchiseptica* and *Pasteurella multocida*. Signs of respiratory disease include nasal discharge, decreased or no appetite, difficulty breathing,

increased breathing sounds, loss of energy and sudden death. Respiratory disease can range from a mild upper respiratory problem to a severe pneumonia. One factor that may make a hedgehog more prone to develop respiratory disease is too low of an environmental temperature. In addition, a poor diet and a dusty or dirty environment can contribute to the development of respiratory disorders. Respiratory disease in the hedgehog can be

rapidly fatal if pneumonia develops, so it is imperative to get your pet to a veterinarian as soon as possible if you see any of the signs listed. Your veterinarian will diagnose respiratory disease based on clinical signs, the physical examination and an X ray. You will need to keep your pet in a warm, quiet, clean area while it is on medication. Exercise should be restricted for hedgehogs with pneumonia until they are back to normal.

Your hedgehog should be free of symptoms such as nasal discharge, decreased appetite, difficulty breathing, increased breathing sounds and loss of energy which indicate respiratory disease.

Other disorders of the hedgehog that can mimic the signs of respiratory disease include heart disease and cancer in the lungs or chest. These can be differentiated from respiratory disease by X ray and/or ultrasound examinations.

UROGENITAL DISEASE

Disease of the urinary system is not commonly recognized in the pet hedgehog. However, these pets can develop bladder infections and stones. Signs of bladder disease may include urine discoloration, straining to urinate, frequent small urination or a complete inability to urinate. In addition, the pain caused by a bladder condition can cause the hedgehog to have a reduced or complete loss of appetite and lethargy. If your pet shows any of these signs you should get it to a veterinarian as soon as possible. Your veterinarian can diagnose bladder disease with a urinalysis and an X ray. A culture of the urine may be done to aid in the selection of an antibiotic. Bladder stones need to be removed surgically. It is important to encourage your hedgehog to drink extra amounts of fluids when treating for bladder disease. It may help to flavor the water with a small amount of one of the products mentioned under the section on medication.

Hedgehogs can develop kidney disease, which becomes more common as the pet ages. Signs of kidney disease can be vague and can include decreased or loss of appetite, wasting, lethargy, decreased or increased urine output and anemia. Kidney disease is diagnosed by a combination of urinalysis and blood tests. In addition, an X ray or ultrasound examination may be helpful.

The most common disease of the reproductive organs, the testicles, uterus and ovaries, is cancer. Hedgehogs can also develop infections of these tissues. Signs of disease in these organs may include infertility, loss of interest in breeding, penile or vaginal discharge, lethargy, loss of appetite and swelling of the abdomen. Disease of the reproductive organs is diagnosed by physical examination, X ray, ultrasound and in some cases by exploratory surgery. The usual recommendation is to remove the affected organ(s) to effectively treat the disease.

GASTROINTESTINAL DISEASE

There is a variety of diseases that afflict the hedgehog's gastrointestinal or digestive tract. One of the more serious is an obstruction of the intestine or stomach with foreign material. Hedgehogs can eat a variety of things in their environment, including pieces of soft rubber toys, other pet's hair and carpet fibers. Since these items are indigestible, they can become lodged at the pylorus (the outflow area of the stomach) or in the intestine. Once this happens, the hedgehog can die in twenty-four to forty-eight hours. Signs of gastrointestinal obstruction include sudden loss of appetite, vomiting (they don't always vomit) and sudden severe lethargy and depression. The condition rapidly worsens until the hedgehog is completely collapsed and comatose. These signs indicate a dire emergency and you must not delay getting your pet to your veterinarian. An X ray will confirm the diagnosis, and exploratory surgery is necessary to remove the foreign material.

Hedgehogs can also develop a number of different infectious diseases of the gastrointestinal tract. The infectious disease of most concern is salmonellosis. Hedgehogs can carry the *Salmonella* spp. bacteria normally in their intestinal tracts (as can other species of animals, most notably, reptiles) and never develop any signs of disease. Hedgehogs can also develop clinical disease from *Salmonella* spp. Signs of salmonellosis include diarrhea, depression, loss of appetite, wasting and sudden death. It is known that humans can contract salmonellosis from hedgehogs. As of this writing, human salmonellosis contracted from African hedgehogs is an extremely rare occurrence, and the chances of transmission are reduced to nearly zero with good hygienic practices as discussed earlier in this chapter. Diagnosis of salmonellosis in the hedgehog with diarrhea is made by a fecal culture. You will need to discuss the treatment options with your veterinarian based on the public health risk for your household. Infants and immune-compromised individuals are most at risk for contracting this or any other disease.

Other conditions of the hedgehog gastrointestinal tract include intestinal parasites, the ingestion of toxic substances, cancer and dietary disease. These diseases can have similar signs including diarrhea or constipation, decreased or absent appetite, wasting, vomiting or lethargy. Your veterinarian can make a diagnosis based on a variety of diagnostic tests including fecal examination, blood tests, X ray, ultrasound and abdominal exploratory.

RABIES

As of this writing, rabies has not been identified in pet African hedgehogs. It is likely that they can contract this disease if exposed to it, but since they are primarily kept inside the house, exposure is minimal. There is currently no approved rabies vaccine for hedgehogs, and it is not recommended to vaccinate them with a dog or cat product. A normal behavior called "self-anointing" is often mistaken for a sign of rabies. (See chapter 1 for a description of self-anointing.)

NUTRITIONAL DISEASE

It is likely that nutritional disease is a much more common problem in the captive African hedgehog than is currently being identified. Extensive nutritional studies have not yet been done in this species, and it is likely that the natural wild diet of the hedgehog is not being 100 percent accurately reproduced in captivity. Subtle nutritional deficiencies or excesses could underlie other diseases. Therefore, it is imperative for you to stay informed on current recommendations for the hedgehog diet by staying in contact with one of the hedgehog organizations and your veterinarian.

One nutritionally related disease that is seen with some frequency is obesity. This is common in hedgehogs that are on a diet too high in fat coupled with a lack of exercise. In addition there is a condition called hepatic lipidosis which is an excessive fat accumulation in the liver. Fat cells replace liver cells until the liver can no longer function normally. The hedgehog becomes lethargic, depressed, loses its appetite and may exhibit bizarre behavior such as seizuring and unusual aggression. These signs are due to the buildup of toxic waste products, such as ammonia, in the blood, which then affect the brain. Liver disease can be diagnosed with blood tests, X rays, ultrasound and liver biopsy if necessary. Treatment for obesity and fatty liver disease is directed at reducing the fat in the diet and increasing exercise. Other medications may be used as needed. Hepatic lipidosis can be reversed if it is caught in time.

Neoplasia (Cancer)

Unfortunately, a large percentage of the captive African hedgehog population is prone to developing cancer as they age. Cancer has been reported affecting almost every organ of the body. Signs of disease vary depending on the area affected. The treatment is based on the organ(s) affected and may even include chemotherapy. It is unknown at this time why African hedgehogs have such a high cancer rate, but perhaps over time the answer will reveal itself as more is learned about this pet.

Alternative Methods of Therapy

There are alternative methods of therapy available for the hedgehog. Discuss these remedies with your veterinarian prior to using them to ensure that there are no potential reactions with the hedgehog's current therapy. For a more detailed discussion of alternative therapies in the hedgehog read *The Natural Hedgehog* which is listed in the reference section.

When It's Time

A well-loved hedgehog is an emotional investment with a world of returns. Unfortunately, there comes a time when every pet owner must say good-bye to a long-time companion and cope with the inevitable loss. The natural reaction to the loss of a pet, a spouse, friend or family member is grief. There is no set way that grief occurs; every person experiences it in his or her unique way. There are varying degrees of intensity and duration for dealing with the sadness of a loss.

There are many ways that people deal with grief. Some find that the best release is a good, hard cry on a friend's shoulder. Others feel better after they have talked about their pet. Sometimes sharing the feelings with someone who has experienced a similar situation is helpful because he or she understands what you are going through.

Enjoying

Your

Hedgehog

Socializing
Your Hedgehog

Once you have allowed your new pet a day or two to settle in, plan to spend at least a half an hour with your hedgehog each day in the first few weeks. You can start by letting your new pet rest in your lap while you watch TV or read. Place your hand near the hedgehog and wait for it to come to investigate. Your hedgehog will gradually learn to relax and explore its immediate surroundings.

Getting to Know Each Other

When you pet your hedgehog, start at the rump and gradually work your way up towards its face. Your hedgehog will be most protective about its face, and it may take several quiet sessions before you are able to touch it near its face and ears. A happy hedgehog will have its spines laid flat and will not feel sharp or prickly. Many hedgehogs will crawl into the crook of your elbow to bury their heads and go back to sleep. They seem to think that if you can't see their face, they are safe!

Give your hedgehog a sense of security by holding it close to your body while speaking in a soothing tone of voice.

Active, well-adjusted hedgehogs will soon be climbing over you to explore. Some can even learn to ride on your shoulder or in a large sweatshirt pocket as you move around your home. As your hedgehog adjusts, you can begin to vary the type of interaction between quiet togetherness and active play.

If you are having trouble getting your pet to adjust, make sure that you are providing adequate exercise in addition to your handling. Hedgehogs who are not getting enough exercise will often be aggressive or agitated and reluctant to relax.

You can provide your hedgehog with supervised playtime on the floor outside the cage and supplement this by giving it access to an exercise wheel. Hedgehogs also love to explore tunnels, boxes, crumpled heaps of paper and mazes. You can also use your old toys to design a play area for your pet. Hedgehogs are good climbers—so make sure your cage or play area has smooth, straight sides or a secure top so that your pet does not escape.

Hedgehogs and Other People

Hedgehogs can distinguish their owners from other people by their scent, voice and attitude. When several

91

members of the same household handle a hedgehog on a regular basis, it will learn to recognize different people and it may react differently to different individuals. Should a stranger attempt to handle the pet, the hedgehog will often keep its quills erect and may even hiss when being handled. If you plan to let other people handle your pet, you will need to put additional effort into conditioning your hedgehog.

The most important thing to remember is that your pet must be relaxed with you before you can expect it to be relaxed with other people. Some hedgehogs can be handled by almost anyone. Others form intense bonds with an individual owner and have a difficult time accepting handling from strangers. You should resist the urge to show your pet off to all of your friends until it has adjusted to you.

Exercise and play-time are essential to the health of your hedgehog.

Once the hedgehog is comfortable with you, invite a friend who enjoys animals to help you begin the socialization process. Have your friend sit in a comfortable position and place the hedgehog in your friend's lap. Your friend should begin the same way you did, letting the hedgehog check things out on its own before attempting to pet or handle the animal. As your pet relaxes, have your friend gently stroke the quills on the rear half of the hedgehog. Repeat this procedure as many times as necessary until your hedgehog has learned to relax quickly. Then, begin to have new people repeat the procedure. You will quickly find out if you have a one-person hedgehog or a gregarious animal that is more interested in play than in who is handling him.

Hedgehogs that Bite

One infrequent, but annoying, problem that can occur with pet hedgehogs is biting. There are two kinds of hedgehog bites. The first type of bite is a playful nip or chewing. Most baby predator animals, includeing humans, will nip as part of the learning process in how to capture food. This should cease once your pet has learned that you are not a food item. The young hedgehog generally starts by licking the object (human or otherwise). The licking becomes more intense and then the hedgehog may actually try to chew on the person or object. It is almost always concluded with a session of self-anointing. The best defense is to recognize when this is happening. When the hedgehog is licking excessively, remove the pet from the object right away.

Men sometimes find the hedgehogs strongly attracted to the salt in their sweat. Women who apply cologne at their wrists are also vulnerable to odor-sensitive hedgehogs. Children who

> **TRICKS TO STOP BITING . . .**
>
> **PREVENTION:**
>
> Gentle handling
>
> Healthy hedgehog
>
> Adequate exercise
>
> **REMEDIES:**
>
> Blowing into the face/nose
>
> Light spray of the face
>
> Drop of rubbing alcohol on nose

have just eaten salty or flavorful snacks are the third most common victim of these playful nips. If you have been wearing leather gloves, you may also find your hands vulnerable. Leather seems to be one of the favorite hedgehog scents. Adults and youngsters alike should get into the practice of washing their hands before handling the family hedgehog to remove potentially attractive odors.

A playful nip is not aggressive in character and does not usually break the skin. The bites feel more like a pinch. While not especially painful, the behavior should be discouraged.

The second type of hedgehog bite is the aggressive or defensive bite. This is a serious problem and much more difficult to deal with than playful nips.

If you have been bitten by your hedgehog, it might be a one-time occurrence for just cause. First-time mothers who are protecting their babies may bite if disturbed, even though these hedgehogs were personal pets and had been handled easily prior to becoming mothers. Hedgehogs that are frightened or in pain may bite to defend themselves. However, the occasional hedgehog develops a bad habit of biting anytime it is handled. If your hedgehog bites repeatedly, you will need to try to cure the habit.

RELEASING A BITE

Should you be bitten by a hedgehog, the hedgehog will usually lock its jaws. When catching prey it does this to hold onto a squirming insect until it can kill it by crushing. The fastest way to get the hedgehog to release a bite hold on your hand is to push your hand toward the back of the hedgehog's jaw. This almost always causes the animal to release the bite. If the bite breaks the skin, wash the wound thoroughly and consult your family physician.

The first step is to make sure that the hedgehog is healthy and not suffering from any condition that might be causing pain. Then make sure that the hedgehog is always handled gently. Frequently, hedgehogs that develop a biting habit have been dropped or roughly handled. Third, make sure that the hedgehog is getting adequate exercise. If there are no obvious reasons for the bites, you can work at trying to cure the habit. Methods that are reported to work include blowing into the hedgehog's nose or face when they bite or spraying the face with a *gentle* plant-mister. Another method that works great is to keep a small bottle of rubbing alcohol around and place a drop on the hedgehog's nose every time it bites. You get IMMEDIATE RELEASE. The hedgehog

---

HEDGEHOG FACTS

DID YOU KNOW THAT YOUR HEDGEHOG...

can be trained to ride in your pocket?

can form an intense bond with you?

loves to play with bright toys?

can be taught to use a litter box?

make interesting noises and even purrs?

---

may anoint, but it is not harmful and they lessen or stop biting.

Occasionally, a hedgehog will have particular preferences, such as preferring women handlers over men. Careful observation can sometimes reveal a pattern to the biting, which can then be used in behavior modification by avoiding the object that is being attacked.

Working with Abused, Frightened or Neglected Hedgehogs

Ideally, a few days of quiet handling is all that is necessary to help your pet adjust to both you and its new home. If, however, you are working with a hedgehog that has been neglected, abused or is very timid, you will find that additional measures must be taken to provide a low-stress experience for the animal. Readers working in animal shelters or other rescue situations are encouraged to read the book *The Natural Hedgehog* (see Chapter 13, "Resources") for a full range of techniques for dealing with neglected or abused hedgehogs.

The first and most important thing when dealing with a frightened or timid hedgehog is that you must be calm and relaxed when you are handling the hedgehog. Slow deep breaths and soft music can help provide a relaxed environment. You need to be able to ignore pressures and deadlines and ringing phones because gaining the hedgehog's trust can take a long time. Hedgehogs respond negatively when their owners are stressed.

This hedgehog has gained enough trust in its human to feel comfortable riding around in a pocket.

95

Some hedgehogs will relax quickly, others may take days or even weeks of quiet handling before they become comfortable enough to venture out of a ball. Signs that the animal is beginning to relax are when it comes out of the balled position and begins to sniff at its surroundings. At this point, the hedgehog should begin to explore your lap cautiously. Once the pet is comfortable with you, begin to gently stroke the quills beginning at the rump and gradually move closer to the face. Be gentle but persistent. If the hedgehog cannot tolerate stroking, set it

Let your hedgehog get comfortable with your scent and touch by placing it on a towel or blanket on your lap until it is ready to explore.

on your arm near the crook of your elbow and again wait for its hissing to stop. Gently scoop it up and move it to a new position. If necessary, pause for the animal to relax again. As the hedgehog learns to trust you and accept handling, gradually increase the amount of contact.

Fun

with Your

Hedgehog

Indoor Playtime

If you enjoy interacting with your hedgehog, you might want to experiment with different things during your indoor play periods. Many hedgehogs can learn to run a maze made of tunnels or blocks, especially when their favorite treat food is used as a reward. Some researchers

and some pet owners have had success teaching their animals to push a colored door open in order to reach their food or treat. This keeps the animal active and helps relieve boredom.

If you find that your hedgehog is not at all interested in play during daylight hours, you can gradually change its feeding time so that it will be more active during the day and go to bed with you at night. Gradually move the feeding back from an evening feeding to about noon. You can also divide the daily diet amount into two or three smaller feedings during the day, beginning in early morning if desired, and provide water and just a tidbit or two at night. The hedgehog will learn to come out during the day to look for food and to spend some time at play, and will sleep through more of the late night hours.

Plan to feed your hedgehog at the time of day you will most often want to play with it if your hours do not coincide with its natural tendency to be up from 7 p.m. to 7 a.m. As long as you make the change gradually, you should be able to adjust its schedule to some extent.

Offer your hedgehog bright plastic toys to push around the indoor play area for exercise and mental stimulation.

Outdoor Playtime

During the summer, many hedgehogs enjoy the opportunity to spend some time outdoors with their owners. If you have a yard and would like to take your pet outdoors, there are just a few precautions that you need to take. First, if you are going to let your hedgehog on the lawn, make sure it has not been recently chemically treated. Even though hedgehogs are supposed to be resistant to many toxins, there have been no documented tests of their reactions to lawn chemicals.

Second, make sure that you place your pet in a secure enclosure. You can move your regular hedgehog cage outside. If your cage is designed with a tray and a wire top, you can often place just the wire top over your pet and weight it with a brick so that your hedgehog can not push it up and escape. If you let your pet loose, remember to watch it at all times. Hedgehogs can run very fast, and if you aren't paying attention to your pet it may be out of sight before you know it.

This hedgehog is enjoying a pile of leaves during some supervised outdoor exploration.

The third precaution is to make sure you have shade and water available for your pet. Small ceramic bowls work well for water and a piece of bark, an old box or a flower pot can provide shelter and shade. A couple of rough stones or bricks provide a climbing toy and help keep the hedgehog's nails worn down.

Fourth, pay attention to changing weather conditions. Please remember that the spot that was cool and shady at ten in the morning may be in the direct sun by noon. In the wild, the hedgehog finds a burrow or pile of grass and leaves to sleep in during the day. This hiding spot protects it from hot sun, cold winds, or rain. In a cage, the hedgehog has no opportunity to escape and find more comfortable accommodations if the weather conditions change. Never leave your pets out overnight or when there is any chance the weather might become cold or rainy. Hedgehogs should not be left outside if the temperature drops below 70 degrees Fahrenheit or goes above 90 degrees Fahrenheit.

Fifth, give your hedgehog some time to adjust. Some hedgehogs love being outdoors and happily begin exploring as soon as they get outside. Others are timid and may simply look for a hiding spot until they adjust. Sometimes they will not become active until dusk when they would wake up under natural conditions.

Your hedgehog can keep you company as you care for your garden, just remember to watch out for what it nibbles on!

Also, stay away from areas used by raccoons for latrines. Raccoon stools contain a parasite that is deadly to hedgehogs and other mammals should they eat it when foraging in the grass. The parasite eggs can stay viable in the soil for *years*. This parasite is called *Baylisascaris procyonis*, raccoon roundworm.

Finally, make sure that your hedgehog is protected from other animals. You may have other pets that get along with your hedgehog, but your neighbor's dog or cat may treat it as interesting prey.

Pet hedgehogs could be offered an opportunity to play in the grass while you garden. Use a secure cage set on the grass near where you are working. The cage can be a simple wooden frame covered with chicken wire with an open bottom that can be placed over the hedgehog. Set a water bowl and hide box in the cage with the hedgehog, add a branch or piece of wood to climb on, then put a weight on the top so that the hedgehog cannot tip the cage up and escape. Some hedgehogs immediately begin tunneling through the grass in search of bugs, others prefer to just nap until dusk. They seem to become most active about the time the evening mosquitoes chase their owners indoors!

If you plan to leave your hedgehog out for prolonged periods of time, you will need to construct a cage with a floor, or bury wire 12 inches (31 centimeters) deep along the sides of the enclosure to keep your pet from burrowing out. You will also want to make sure that it is sturdy enough to keep predators out. A small shrub or two will provide an alternative sleep site during the day if your hedgehog does not wish to use its nest box.

Besides being adorable, hedgehogs are also useful for bringing stories to life for children.

Volunteering with Your Hedgehog

If you enjoy reading and have a sociable hedgehog, you might consider conducting a hedgehog story hour at your local library, school, or youth organization. Select a book aimed at the age level of the children for whom you will be reading. There are a number of good books listed in Chapter 12, "Recommended Reading." Read the book several times in advance. How does the behavior and appearance of the hedgehog in the book compare to your pet? What hedgehog trait or myth does the book deal with? Think of some questions to ask during your program.

One way to begin a program is to use a blackboard or flip chart and ask the children what they know about hedgehogs. Discuss what is myth and what is true. Sometimes your first question will be "Why isn't your hedgehog blue like Sonic?" Now, read the book you have selected and then show the group your own hedgehog. Answer any questions they have. If you decide to let the children handle or pet your hedgehog, remember to have them wash their hands (or use baby wipes or other wash ups) before and after handling the hedgehog. Washing their hands in advance helps prevent your hedgehog from smelling and trying to *taste* their lunch! Washing their hands afterward is a good sanitary measure to prevent the itching reaction sometimes encountered after contact with hedgehog quills. This also teaches children good hygiene when handling pets and prevents the slight possibility of disease transmission.

After you have finished your program, ask the children what new information they learned about hedgehogs that they did not know before the program.

This type of program takes a minimum amount of preparation, but can be a lot of fun if you enjoy children and like to educate them about hedgehogs.

Photo Sessions, Special Events and Competitions

You can take lots of cute pictures with your hedgehog if it has been socialized and is comfortable with handling. Hedgehogs have helped owners win awards for photography and writing, either in school, in 4-H and scouting programs or in community sponsored competition and county fairs.

A topic that will be of interest to your local newspaper is that February 2 each year is Hedgehog Day. You can share the history of this event with the media. Hedgehogs were predicting the weather for the Romans long before they were replaced by the North American groundhog! Contact the newspaper in early

January and ask if they would be interested in a short article. Many editors are delighted and will even send a photographer out to take pictures of you and your pet.

One veterinarian works with his hedgehog clients on a special hedgehog day program each year. He offers free health checkups for hedgehogs on February 2 or the closest business day to the holiday. A local hedgehog breeder brings in two or three socialized hedgehogs to use for demonstrations on routine grooming. It provides publicity for the veterinarian's practice, plus area hedgehog owners get a chance to meet each other and share interesting hedgehog stories. This idea may work well for your local veterinarian.

Hedgehogs make great subjects for cute photographs! Many owners enter community competitions with the help of their pet.

Another event that is popular with hedgehog owners are pet parades. It is a wonderful place to show off your hedgehog to a large group of people. Some hedgehog owners even create special habitats or a carrier with a theme just for a parade. Watch your local newspaper or the bulletin board at your library or park district for a notice of this type of event in your community.

HEDGEHOG SHOWS

In some parts of the United States and Canada it is now possible to show your hedgehog in competition against other hedgehogs, much as you would show your rabbit, dog or horse. Some hedgehog shows judge only the quality of the animal based on a published standard for color, conformation and temperament.

103

Other shows also offer judging for decorated hedgehog habitats. The organizations sponsoring the shows
often schedule seminars on hedgehog care and breeding along with the show, so it can be both a fun and
educational event. If you are interested in showing
your pet, contact the North American Hedgehog
Association or International Hedgehog Fancier's
Society (see Chapter 13, "Resources") for the location
of the closest club events.

Traveling with Your Hedgehog

When transporting your hedgehog, use your common
sense to help ensure that your pet is safe and comfortable. First, select an appropriate carrier. A small plastic
or soft sided pet carrier works well. Select one that is
comfortable for your pet and
easy for you to carry. In the car,
give some thought to the place-
ment of the carrier. Keep it out
of direct sunlight on hot days
and do not put it directly in front
of an open air-conditioning vent.
Never leave your pet in the car
on a hot day. Even though hedgehogs enjoy warm weather, a
closed car will quickly become
too hot and can result in heat
stroke or death.

In cold weather, make sure your
pet has plenty of fluffy bedding
to snuggle in. If you need to take
your pet out in cold weather,
place a hot water bottle or one of

*A portable plas-
tic carrier for car
travel should be
placed in a safe
position out of
direct sunlight.*

the small hand-warmer packets sold for sportsmen
inside an old sock and place that in the carrier. Make
sure the hedgehog has enough room to move away
from the hand-warmer should it be too hot for the
hedgehog. Take the time to warm up the car before
transporting your hedgehog. You can also cover your
carrier with a blanket or towel when moving from the
house to the car.

Be prepared for any type of delay by bringing along some of your hedgehog's supplies from home. A ration of its favorite dry food is essential as well as some treat items, like bits of fruit and vegetables. Don't forget to bring the water bottle from home, as familiar water will ensure that your hedgehog will accept drinking from it because it smells familiar.

> ## TRAVELING SAFETY TIPS
>
> • Select a safe pet carrier
>
> • Stabilize the carrier during travel
>
> • Keep the carrier out of direct sunlight
>
> • Allow for adequate ventilation
>
> • Never leave your pet in the car unattended

If you plan to take your pet on vacation and you are flying, make sure that you contact the airline about their carry-on pet policy in advance. Only a few of the major airlines will allow your pet to travel under your seat and there is always an additional charge. Make sure that if your hedgehog is placed in cargo, that it will be riding in a temperature controlled compartment.

Air travel is stressful for most animals, and I do not recommend taking your pet on this kind of vacation if you can arrange for its care while you are out of town. Hedgehogs are best left in their own homes, or at least in their own cages at the home of the caretaker, while you are on vacation.

Hedgehog Folktales, Myths and Mysteries

Hedgehogs have been part of legend and folklore throughout their range for thousands of years. One of the most interesting bits of history is that surrounding Hedgehog Day. In the United States and Canada, February 2 is celebrated as Groundhog Day. People watch zoo groundhogs on that date to see whether or not they see their shadow. If the groundhog sees its shadow and returns to its burrow, there is to be six more weeks of winter. Historically, however, February 2 is Hedgehog Day.

Hedgehog Day

Hedgehog Day began centuries ago as part of the festival of *Februa*. The Romans observed that the hedgehog hibernated and originated the weather myth that if the hedgehog comes out of its den on

February 2 and sees its shadow, it means there is a clear moon and six more weeks of winter will follow. Although the Romans were smart enough to realize that hedgehogs venture out at night and not in the sun, the hedgehogs' weather predicting abilities are more myth than fact.

In Britain in the fifth century, the Christian festival of Candlemas began to replace the Roman festival of *Februa* on February 2, and the Christians added their own twist to the weather prediction: If Candlemas be fair, there be two winters in the year. Although Candlemas ignored the hedgehog, tradition and the myth did not fade completely, and St. Dubricious, a fifth-century saint, is shown with a hedgehog at his feet in the stained glass window of Gloucestshire's Hentland Church in the United Kingdom.

Over the next fifteen centuries, the hedgehog weather myth gradually faded, although hedgehogs continued to appear in literature, on coins and later on stamps. There is a heraldic shield emblazoned with hedgehogs on one of the garden walls of Canterbury Cathedral in the United Kingdom.

Hedgehogs are the originators of the weather myth.

While the hedgehog's role as a weather forecaster diminished in Britain, it reappeared in a new guise in North America: Groundhog Day. As people emigrated from Britain to the US and Canada, they brought the myth along. Since there were no hedgehogs, they substituted a furry rodent, the groundhog, for the prickly insectivore of their homeland. Now each year the Canadians with "Wiarton Willie" and the Americans in Pennsylvania with "Punxsutawney Phil" duke it out over who started Groundhog Day. The celebrations are hardly reminiscent of hedgehogs under a clear moon!

107

APPLE LOVERS?

Another European myth surrounding the hedgehog is that hedgehogs would roll onto apples, stick them to their spines and then carry them back to their burrows to eat. This was apparently originally written down by Pliney more than 2,000 years ago and appears in almost every hedgehog book. In looking at reproductions of old woodcuts and drawings of hedgehogs and apples, it is likely that the apples are really crab apples or perhaps grapes or ripe figs. Many hedgehogs do like the taste of apples and grapes, but it is probably more likely that the hedgehogs were rolling in rotting fruit or self-anointing so that the quills were sticky than that they intentionally harvested apples for future use. Although hedgehogs may eat fruit, it is rare for them to consume a significant quantity, and no field study has revealed any tendency to store food. Pat Morris demonstrated on a BBC wildlife program, *The Great Hedgehog Mystery*, that one can stick a mushy apple forcefully onto the back of a bristling hedgehog and it will stay put while it walks around, but to duplicate such an event in nature would require rather unusual circumstances. The curious appearance and apparently eccentric behavior of the hedgehog has often lent itself to misunderstandings.

Rooting is one hedgehog behavior that has been the subject of folktales.

The Misunderstood Hedgehog

Another misunderstanding is that hedgehogs routinely carry rabies. The act of foaming at the mouth has historically been associated with rabid animals. During self-anointing, hedgehogs produce huge quantities of frothy saliva which they spread liberally across their quills. This makes the foamy saliva readily visible to even a casual observer. While a few individual animals may actually have contracted and spread rabies, it is likely that the majority of those so accused were merely practicing one of their favorite habits.

During the reign of Queen Elizabeth I, the life of a misunderstood hedgehog, such as this African Pygmy, was sought for threepence.

Hedgehogs have attracted unfavorable attention from humans for other reasons as well. They were persecuted and killed by the thousands in some parts of Britain and Europe with bounties paid for the skins in many areas. In 1566 during the reign of Queen Elizabeth I, churchwardens were authorized to pay out threepence for every hedgehog killed throughout the realm according to the Preservation of Grayne act. This law listed a number of animals, including the hedgehog, as vermin responsible for the destruction of agricultural interests. Gamekeepers exterminated them in an effort to protect game birds' eggs and chicks, even though it was never demonstrated that they were responsible for sufficient losses to justify the sustained and extensive campaign against them. In other areas, hedgehogs were thought to be carriers of the plague because they were so often infested with fleas. Ironically, today the hedgehog is a protected species in almost all of the same countries that once persecuted it.

Nothing was going right for the hedgehog in England during the Middle Ages. Even his old English name, urchone or urchin, meant a kind of elf or troublesome sprite. Shakespeare may actually have helped in a small way by popularizing the word hedgehog.

This plump hedgehog might be considered a gustatory treat in South Africa.

One of the well-known and more practical uses for hedgehogs was as a tasty meal. A fat hedgehog is still regarded as a tasty treat in South Africa, and, as a result, *A. frontalis* is threatened in part of its range. In years past gypsies dined off them regularly, attaching curative powers to various parts of the hedgehog's anatomy. Fat animals caught in the autumn as they were preparing to hibernate were especially favored. The usual description was that the animal was rolled in clay and roasted or baked. When the clay covering was removed, the spines would be removed, embedded in the clay.

Hedgehogs were also used in the preparations of all kinds of medicines that were held to cure just about every human ailment. Among the hedgehog remedies described in Middle Ages medical texts,

---

THE HARE AND THE HEDGEHOG

This modern children's video reworks the traditional tale, *The Tortoise and the Hare*. It centers around the life of a small hedgehog who tries to teach his son how to avoid confrontations, but then, in a fit of pride, finds himself challenging a rabbit to a race. Being considerably slower than the rabbit, the hedgehog resorts to cleverness to win, and in the process teaches himself and his son a few important lessons in life. In the race of life, a strong and clever mind wins over a strong pair of legs.

hedgehog ashes were good for boils and the powdered skin of the hedgehog could stop hair from falling out. The hedgehog's right eye, fried in linseed oil and drunk from a brass vessel would improve night vision. Concoctions of dried rib skin and herbs were prescribed for colic.

Some of the more practical uses to which people put hedgehogs were to use the dried and stretched skins for carding wool and dressing flax. The spines dried like a bed of fine nails and were useful for combing out these fibers. Farmers also used them on the top rails of their orchard fences to keep out small boys and coachmen attached them to carriage shafts to prevent their horses from dozing on the job.

Hedgehogs are a favorite subject for craft work.

In European folklore, hedgehogs have long been accused of suckling dairy cows, supposedly reducing milk yields and helping to spread foot and mouth disease. It is unlikely, however, that a hedgehog could fit a cow's nipple into its mouth and suckle effectively, although they might lick drops of milk leaking onto the ground. Most cows would not tolerate the attentions of a suckling hedgehog. Les Stocker, founder of St. Tiggywinkle's Hedgehog Hospital, suggests that perhaps the hedgehogs might actually try to eat the nipples of recumbent cows since they will generally try to eat any animal flesh that presents itself. The distress caused to the cow by a gnawing hedgehog could indeed reduce milking performance.

Beloved Hedgehogs

Few Europeans spoke up for hedgehogs until the middle to late nineteenth century, but in other cultures or during other periods hedgehogs were regarded as *good* symbols of various sorts. Norwegians, for example, held the hedgehog as the symbol of independent thinkers. And the ancient Chinese civilization in the He Bei Province regarded their resident hedgehogs as sacred.

The hedgehog is a well-loved character in Latvian folktales. The Latvians frequently used hedgehogs in their traditional charm whistles, or *Svilpaunicki*. To make a sound was to bring good luck, and the whistle with an animal was an ancient theme that was the embodiment of luck. The hedgehog is most often portrayed as an underdog who suffers tremendous trials and tribulations but never gives up. The hedgehog is the symbol for perseverance. Not necessarily obtaining everything it wants, it nevertheless continues in pursuit of its goals and triumphs in the end.

In more modern tales, Sonic the Hedgehog in his bright blue quills blazes across the screen on cartoons and video games. In reality, hedgehogs are fast for their size and have been clocked at speeds of up to 6 feet per second for short distances. Sonic, of course, can easily beat this and his color has prompted countless children to inquire why hedgehogs aren't blue like Sonic.

SHAKESPEARE'S TAKE ON HEDGEHOGS

Shakespeare was among the many authors of the time to depict the "hedgehogs are vermin" cause. He described Richard III as a hedgehog, obviously meaning something verminous:

Dost thou grant me hedgehog? Then God grant me too
Thou mayst be dammed for the wicked deed!

Later in *A Midsummer Night's Dream* he slandered hedgehogs and other animals with:

You spotted snakes with double tongue,
Thorny hedgehogs, be not seen;
Newts and blindworms, do no wrong;
Come not near our Fairy Queen.

LITERARY HEDGEHOGS

In the literary world, the two most famous hedgehog appearances are Beatrix Potter's washerwoman, Mrs.

Tiggywinkle, and the rolled up hedgehog used as a croquet ball in Lewis Carroll's *Alice In Wonderland*. The hedgehog was an odd choice for a washerwoman and Alice certainly had her hands full, both with using a flamingo as a mallet and with the hedgehogs getting stuck in furrows or running away in the middle of the game.

In more recent years, the hedgehog has appeared in several dozen children's stories, usually portrayed as an inoffensive, no nonsense type of character. One character who is an exception to this is the Jim Hedgehog character in children's stories by Russell Hoban. Jim's big appetite in *Jim Hedgehog's Supernatural Christmas* and his curious exploring in *Jim Hedgehog and the Lonesome Tower* leads him into all kinds of trouble.

In addition to books, images of hedgehogs can now be found as door stops, plastic toys for dogs and cats in neon colors, figurines, stationery, greeting cards, stuffed toys, dolls, shirts, jewelry and so on in an almost endless list. Many people collect anything and everything resembling a hedgehog until they fill whole rooms with "hedgehogabilia!"

In any language, hedgehogs make beloved pets.

Today hedgehogs in the United Kingdom enjoy the care and protection of several organizations that have made hedgehog preservation a major concern. The best known is St. Tiggywinkle's Hedgehog Hospital in Aylesbury, Bucks, England where Les and Sue Stocker and their staff treat hundreds of injured hedgehogs each year before returning the rehabilitated animals to the wild. Other lesser-known hospitals

Enjoying Your
Hedgehog

conduct hedgehog rehabilitation on a smaller scale throughout the country. Another well-known organization is the British Hedgehog Preservation Society, a group which educates people about hedgehogs. The interest in these adorable little creatures has introduced many people to conservation and the safety of wildlife in urbanized areas.

HEDGEHOGS AND CROP CIRCLES

Some reference works on unidentified flying objects state that one explanation for the crop circles in England is that they are caused by rampant hedgehogs. Watching hedgehogs run laps in their cages or on their wheels, one can only imagine what wonders they might create in somebody's wheat field. Still, if you look at photos of crop circles you would need a tremendous herd of a normally solitary animal to create such patterns!

NAMES FOR HEDGEHOGS IN VARIOUS LANGUAGES

This listing of names for hedgehogs may be entertaining to hedgehog owners and useful for those searching international sources for literature on hedgehogs.

Africaanse	krimpvarkie
Chinese	ci-wei (needle animal)
French	herisson
German	igel
Irish	grainneog
Latin	erinaceus, ericius or echinus
Spanish	erizo

114

Legal Issues of Hedgehog Ownership

Once you have decided that you want to purchase a hedgehog as a pet, you need to consider the legality of owning a hedgehog. In 1990, the United States Department of Agriculture banned imports of hedgehogs from Africa for health and political reasons. The species *Atelerix*

frontalis is already regarded as threatened, due to its popularity as a pet and as a food delicacy in South Africa. Fortunately, there were enough hedgehogs already in the United States to ensure an adequate breeding population. Through the efforts of a handful of breeders, the hedgehog was successfully bred domestically and its future secured as a pet. Through good nutrition, veterinary care and judicious breeding, the United States and Canadian hedgehog herds are now the largest in the world and hedgehogs are even shipped overseas from American breeders on a regular basis.

Although much has changed since the early years of hedgehog breeding in the US, and even though pet African hedgehogs are domestically raised, they are still classified as exotic, nondomestic animals by most government agencies. This will not change because no species of hedgehog is indigenous (native) to the United States or Canada.

Hedgehog Restrictions

At the time of the writing of this book, it is still illegal to own hedgehogs in California and Arizona, and some other states require permits or have other restrictions on the ownership of hedgehogs. In addition, some cities within "hedgehog legal" states do not permit hedgehogs or have special requirements for their ownership. Some states do not permit hedgehogs and various other exotic animals because they are afraid that they might get loose and naturalize. This argument is sometimes supported by the case of the successful introduction of the European hedgehogs in New Zealand. Most of the hedgehogs sold in the US and Canada are the African type, and it is doubtful that they could survive if released due to their particular temperature requirements. They could, however, survive in some parts of the southwestern United States. In most countries, hedgehogs are considered beneficial because they consume large quantities of creatures considered to be vermin, but in other areas they are considered pests.

It is important to check with your local animal control officer before purchasing a hedgehog. Your animal control officer will be able to tell you if it is legal to own a hedgehog in your community and if any permits are necessary. If you keep a hedgehog in a state or community that forbids it, you can be arrested or fined and your pet can be confiscated and possibly euthanized. Be aware that just because a local pet shop may be selling hedgehogs does not mean that they may be kept in your locality. Please check with your community *before* you purchase a pet.

If your community does not have an animal control officer, or the officer is not sure of the status of hedgehogs, check with your state or provincial government. In the United States, the agencies responsible for regulating pets vary. The first agencies to try would be the state departments of agriculture, natural resources, conservation, or fish and wildlife.

Don't fall outside the law. Responsible pet ownership begins with understanding and abiding by federal and local regulations for hedgehogs.

Federal Restrictions

At the present time, there are no federal restrictions on hedgehog ownership in the United States. However, should you decide to become a breeder and sell your surplus hedgehogs, you may be required to obtain a license from the United States Department of Agriculture (USDA). At the time this book was written, individuals who plan to sell hedgehogs on a wholesale basis and those who wish to exhibit hedgehogs on a fee basis are required to obtain federal licenses.

117

If you live in an area that forbids hedgehog ownership and decide to work to change their legal status,
contact one of the associations listed in Chapter 13,
"Resources." They will be able to assist you and provide information that will be helpful in working with
your local or state authorities.

Beyond the Basics

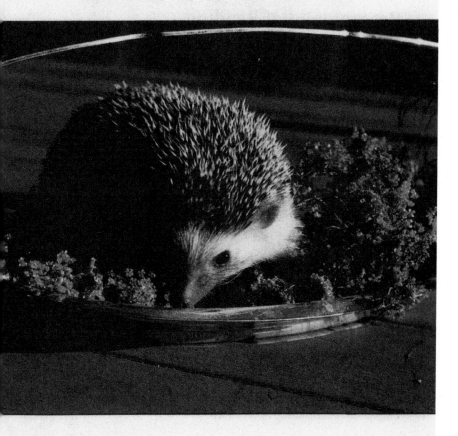

Resources

Recommended Reading

BOOKS

Health & Care

Carpenter, James W., DVM, Mashima, Ted Y., DVM, and David J. Rupiper, DVM. *Exotic Animal Formulary*. Philadelphia, Pennsylvania: WB Saunders, Co., 2001.

Kelsey-Wood, Dennis. *African Pygmy Hedgehogs as Your New Pet*. Neptune, New Jersey: TFH Publications, 1995.

Reeve, Nigel. *Hedgehogs: (T & Ad Natural History Series)*. San Diego, California: Academic Press, 1996.

MAGAZINES

The Following Magazines Occasionally Cover Topics Relevant to Hedgehogs:

Critters (annual)
Fancy Publications
3 Burroughs Dr.
Irvine, CA 92618
(949) 855-8822
(800) 361-4132
www.animalnetwork.com

Animals Exotic & Small (bi-monthly)
NBAF Magazine Subscriptions
161 W. University Parkway, Box 12225
Jackson, TN 38308-10137
Fax: (731) 668-7300
E-mail: sales@nbaf.com
http://nbaf.com/subscriptions/ho/aes.html

Rare Breeds Journal
P.O. Box 66
Crawford, NE 69339
(308) 665-1431
Fax: (308) 665-1931
E-mail: RBJ@rarebreedsjournal.com
www.rarebreedsjournal.com

Websites

Ain't No Creek Ranch, Inc.
www.aintnocreek.com

This website has lots of attitude and many hedgehog-related goods. Visit to sign up for "Go Hog Wild!" the world's largest all-hedgehog event. Or logon to view the "Spike and Friends Collection" if you are interested in purchasing a hedgie, buying specialized hedgehog food, cages, exercise equipment or toys. There's also plenty for the hedgie-loving human, including hedgehog jewelry and T-shirts. Please note that Ain't No Creek Ranch provides information on a variety of small animals, so make sure that you're in the hedgehog site—you don't want to accidentally order chinchilla food for your hedgie now, do you?

The Flying Hedgehog
www.hedgehog.org

If you're ready to bring a hedgehog into your life, this is the site to discover information on breeders, including where in the United States hedgehogs are legal or are restricted. Breeder contact information is provided, as are a color flow chart and a list of other insectivores (insect eaters).

Hedgehogs—Animal Hospitals—USA
www.animalhospitals-usa.com/small_pets/
hedgehogs.html

Visit this user-friendly website and discover how to choose a healthy hedgehog. An extensive checklist provides descriptions of proper eye, ear, nose and quill health, along with the kind of temperament that you should look for in a well-adjusted hedgehog.

The Hedgehog Catalog
www.massena.com/sharon/hhcatalog.htm

For the ultimate in one stop shopping, visit the Hedgehog Catalog. Click on hedgies to choose from a plethora of goods, including stationary, jewelry, decorative items, key chains, teapots, mugs—even an adorable hedgie doormat. More serious, cage and care-related items are also highlighted.

The Hedgehog Fact Sheets
www.hedgehogs.org.uk/facts

This British website provides a straightforward array of information on caring for a sick hedgie. CRASH (Care, Rehabilitation and Aid for Sick Hedgehogs), at the Hedgehog Hospital, provides instructions on what to do when you see a hedgie out during the day, or when a hedgie is suffering from possible pesticide contamination. Other topics covered include hedgie hibernation, the question of whether hedgehogs are intelligent and do they have fleas?

Hedgehog FAQ: Care and Understanding
www.cs.ruu.nl/wais/html/na-dir/
hedgehog-faq/part5.html

This very up-to-date website contains seven significant sections, including behavior (which covers self-anointing—what it is and why hedgehogs do it), health care, problems to watch for—such as a wobbly hedgehog—and "Things Hedgehogs say and do."

The Hedgehog Hobby Homepage
http://keremeos.net/hedgehoghobby/
introduction.html

A visit to this key site is a must for hedgie hobbyists. This website covers the many reasons for adoring hedgehogs, from their friendly and inquisitive nature to their smiling expressions. Another significant fact— that hedgies don't smell—is heavily promoted here. Links are provided for more information on quills, health, hibernation, daily routine and dental care.

Hedgehogs in the Garden
www.overthegardengate.net/wildlife/hedgehog.asp

This site concentrates on hedgies as expert gardeners. If you think that good help is hard to find, you've never met a hedgehog. Hedgies operate quietly as they eat bugs—but not your garden's furnishings. Because they are so quiet, this site recommends that you check your garden twice before shoveling, lest you dig up your slumbering hedgie.

Hedgehog Valley (Tig's Hedgehog Page)
http://members.tripod.com/~antigonemeans/index.html

From Hedgehog Valley, Kansas, comes this charming, family-oriented site. Visit this USDA licensed hedgehog breeder if you want to purchase a baby hedgie or adopt an adult. The site also contains information on hedgehog health and veterinary care issues, including a section on obesity.

The International Hedgehog Club
www.hedgehogclub.com

The website for the International Hedgehog Association promotes proper hedgehog care to an international audience. This non-profit organization helps in the rescue, welfare, support and care of hedgehogs everywhere.

The Small Animal Pages: Welcome, Hedgehog Aficionados!
www.pet-net.net/small_animals/hedgehogs.htm

Visit this website, and soon you'll be whisked to Hedgehog information centers, chat groups, Web rings, and much more—each neatly organized by subject area!

VetCentric: All about hedgehogs
www.vetcentric.com/magazine/
magazineArticle.cfm?ARTICLEID=1101

For a veterinary perspective on hedgehogs, visit this website. There is nothing new here, but all the information is presented clearly and concisely.

The Virtual Hedgehog Show Site
http://hedghogshow.com

If you can't make it to a live hedgehog show, this virtual one should do just fine. Among the rules and regulations, your hedgehog must be properly entered into the competition (sending in a photograph will do). Competing categories include Memorial class—for dear departed hedgies—a Differently-abled Hog class and the ever-snappy Costume class.

WHS: Wobbly Hedgehog Syndrome
www.angelfire.com/wa2/comemeetmyfamily/wob-blyhs1.html

This website contains extensive information on Wobbly Hedgehog Syndrome (WHS). WHS is a hedgehog illness that mimics Multiple Sclerosis in humans. There are no known cures for WHS, but there are treatments that may help extend your hedgie's life. Diet is especially important. Give your hedgehog fresh, live insects along with the appropriate, veterinarian-recommended vitamin supplements. Massage is also beneficial. You might even want to create an area in your home where your hedgehog can "walk" and support himself—this may mean creating narrow walkways in your hedgie's cage so that he can brace himself as he moves along. Comfortable accommodations, including pillows and blankets, will keep your hedgie warm and cozy. And be sure that he has plenty of water to drink.

The Welsh Hedgehog Hospital
www.whh.org

To purchase a proper hedgehog house, check out homeopathic hedgie remedies or to glance at quirky illustrations of a hedgehog-friendly garden, be sure to stop by this site.

Associations and Clubs

International Hedgehog Fanciers Society (IHFS)
P.O. Box 1417
Oroville, WA 98844-1217
In Canada
P.O. Box 426
Keremeos, BC V0X IN0

The IHFS was the first organization in the world to design a comprehensive standard, judging, and exhibition system for hedgehogs. The IHFS publishes a monthly newsletter, Hedgehog Central, and sponsors local and regional clubs and a 4-H youth program. For help in finding a club near you, contact the IHFS or the NAHA (below).

North American Hedgehog Association (NAHA)
601 Tijeras NW #201
Albuquerque, NM 87102
(505) 842-1535
Fax: (505) 842-8560

The NAHA was established in 1993 to serve the needs of those who share an interest in owning, breeding and living with domestic hedgehogs. They publish the *Hedgehog World* newsletter along with pamphlets on hedgehog selection, care and handling.

Mail-Order Sources for Information and Supplies

Absorption Corporation
1051 Hilton Ave.
Bellingham, WA 98225
(800) 242-2287
E-mail: absorbs@absorption-corp.com
www.socksandpads.com

Absorption Corp. offers bedding products for hedgehogs.

Brisky Pet Products
P.O. Box 186
South Main St.
Franklinville, NY 14737
(800) 462-2462
Fax: (716) 557-2336
E-mail: sales@brisky.com
www.brisky.com

Brisky supplies low-iron hedgehog food along with other items.

Hinestein Exotic Pets
11961 South Emerson Rd.
Canby, OR 97013
(503) 263-8886
Fax (503) 262-8885
E-mail: exclheggie@aol.com

Contact Hinestein for hedgehog exercise wheels, housing, collectibles and low-iron hedgehog food.

HABA Exotic Animal Enclosures
17837 1st Ave. S., Suite 525
Seattle, WA 98148
(206) 244-0285
Fax: (206) 248-7205
E-mail: gencinc@uswest.net
www.habaexotic.com

If you're looking for hedgie nest boxes or habitats, get in touch with HABA.

Mountain Meadows Pet Products, Inc.
P.O. Box 778
Lewiston, MT 59457
(800) 752-8864
Fax: (406) 538-2545
E-mail: mmeadows@tein.net
www.mtnmeadowspet.com/default/htm

Mountain Meadows provides safe and biodegradable hedgie products.

CPSIA information can be obtained
at www.ICGtesting.com
Printed in the USA
BVOW07*1413160617
487112BV00001B/1/P